OECD Public Governance Reviews

Strengthening Public Integrity in Brazil

MAINSTREAMING INTEGRITY POLICIES IN THE FEDERAL EXECUTIVE BRANCH

This document, as well as any data and map included herein, are without prejudice to the status of or sovereignty over any territory, to the delimitation of international frontiers and boundaries and to the name of any territory, city or area.

Please cite this publication as:
OECD (2021), *Strengthening Public Integrity in Brazil: Mainstreaming Integrity Policies in the Federal Executive Branch*, OECD Public Governance Reviews, OECD Publishing, Paris, *https://doi.org/10.1787/a8cbb8fa-en*.

ISBN 978-92-64-84049-2 (print)
ISBN 978-92-64-99675-5 (pdf)

OECD Public Governance Reviews
ISSN 2219-0406 (print)
ISSN 2219-0414 (online)

Photo credits: Cover © Adalberto Carvalho Pinto-Assessoria de Comunicação Social da Controladoria-Geral da União. (Se precisar do cargo: Auditor Federal de Finanças e Controle).

Corrigenda to publications may be found on line at: *www.oecd.org/about/publishing/corrigenda.htm*.
© OECD 2021

The use of this work, whether digital or print, is governed by the Terms and Conditions to be found at *http://www.oecd.org/termsandconditions*.

Foreword

Integrity in the public service is vital to ensure that resources are used to serve the public interest and pursue the government's policy goals. Ultimately, integrity policies seek to promote the application of shared values and to achieve sustainable change in organisational cultures in the public administration and in the behaviour of public servants. Without such change, integrity policies may end up existing primarily on paper or, at best, becoming a check-the-box exercise of ensuring compliance with regulations and standards without real ownership and commitment.

Public sector entities vary widely in terms of their mandates, resources and capacities, as well as the context operate in and the integrity risks they face. A strategic vision of public integrity therefore avoids a one-size-fits-all approach, allows public entities to set relevant and realistic objectives and prioritises actions based on actual integrity risks and opportunities.

In Brazil, a federal country with a complex and diverse public administration, implementing such a strategic vision can be a challenge, as it requires mainstreaming integrity regulations and policies throughout the public administration, ensuring that standards are met, promoting coherence and avoiding mixed messages to public servants, whilst acknowledging differences and allowing public entities to adapt to their specific characteristics.

This report is part of an ongoing project through which the OECD provides support to the Office of the Comptroller General of the Union, which leads integrity policies at the federal level, in strengthening its policies, methods and institutions to promote integrity in the federal executive branch. The project has three components: a review of the integrity risk assessment methodology; the application of behavioural insights to public integrity; and strengthening the Integrity Management Units (UGI). In July 2021, during the implementation of this project, Brazil established the Public Integrity System of the Federal Executive Branch (SIPEF) and the UGI became the sectorial units of this new system, directed by the CGU. The scope of this report subsequently broadened to look not only at the UGI but at the SIPEF and the CGU as its central organ.

This report contributes to OECD work to support countries in effectively implementing the *OECD Recommendation on Public Integrity*. It provides concrete recommendations on how to strengthen the Brazilian integrity system at the federal level by improving the coherence and the visibility of integrity in view of offering better guidance to public servants. As such, its findings and recommendations can also inspire other countries facing similar issues. In addition, this report provides an input to the forthcoming *OECD Integrity Review of Brazil*.

The review was approved by the OECD Working Party of Senior Public Integrity Officials (SPIO) on 11 November 2021 and declassified by the Public Governance Committee on 3 December 2021.

Acknowledgements

The report was prepared by the OECD Public Sector Integrity Division of the Directorate for Public Governance under the direction of Elsa Pilichowski, OECD Director for Public Governance and Julio Bacio Terracino, Acting Head of the Public Sector Integrity Division. The report was co-ordinated and drafted by Frédéric Boehm. Giulio Nessi, Carissa Munro, Maria Camila Porras, Camila Gomes and Laura Uribe provided invaluable support and inputs. Alessandro Bellantoni, David Goessmann, Emma Cantera and Claire McEvoy provided feedback. The report was peer-reviewed by Izadora Zubek, from the French Anti-corruption Agency (Agence Française Anticorruption, AFA), who provided invaluable comments and inputs to strengthen the analysis and the recommendations. Editorial and administrative assistance was provided by Meral Gedik. The Portuguese translation of the report was prepared by Pedro Milliet and edited in depth by Camila Gomes and Carolina Souto Carballido.

The OECD thanks the Minister of the Office of the Comptroller General of the Union (*Controladoria-Geral da União*, CGU), Wagner de Campos Rosário, as well as his staff, in particular the Secretariat of Transparency and Corruption Prevention (*Secretaria de Transparência e Prevenção da Corrupção*, STPC), Claudia Taya and Roberto Cesar de Oliveira Viegas, the Directorate for Integrity Promotion (*Diretoria de Promoção da Integridade*, DPI), Pedro Ruske Freitas and Carolina Souto Carballido, for their support in organising the virtual fact-finding and for the many fruitful discussions on preliminary findings and recommendations throughout the project.

The OECD would also like to thank the individuals and organisations who took part in the process and provided valuable information for the preparation of the report. In particular, the OECD is grateful for the feedback and information shared by the Technical secretariat of the Public Ethics Commission (Comissão de Ética Pública, CEP) and the Integrity Management Units of the following federal entities that participated in the Focus Group and bilateral interviews: National Agency for Telecommunications (*Agência Nacional de Telecomunicações*), National Department of Transport Infrastructure (*Departamento Nacional de Infraestrutura de Transportes*), Ministry of Citizenship (*Ministério da Cidadania*), Ministry of Women, Family and Human Rights (*Ministério da Mulher, da Família e dos Direitos Humanos*), Ministry of Agriculture, Livestock and Supply (*Ministério da Agricultura, Pecuária e Abastecimento*), Ministry of Education (*Ministério da Educação*), Federal University of Maranhão Foundation (*Fundação Universidade Federal do Maranhão*), Federal Institute of Education, Science and Technology of Santa Catarina (*Instituto Federal de Educação, Ciência e Tecnologia de Santa Catarina*), National Film Agency (*Agência Nacional do Cinema*), Brazilian Institute for the Environment and Renewable Natural Resources (*Instituto Brasileiro do Meio Ambiente e dos Recursos Naturais Renováveis*), Ministry of Infrastructure (*Ministério da Infraestrutura*), Ministry of Tourism (*Ministério do Turismo*), General Secretariat of the Presidency of the Republic (*Secretaria-Geral da Presidência da República*), National Health Foundation (*Fundação Nacional de Saúde*), Superintendence for the Development of the Midwest (*Superintendência de Desenvolvimento do Centro-Oeste*), Ministry of Economy (*Ministério da Economia*) and Office of the Comptroller General of the Union (*Controladoria-Geral da União*). Finally, the OECD thanks the 30 Integrity Management Units that provided answers to the questionnaire sent out in 2020.

Table of contents

Foreword	3
Acknowledgements	4
Executive summary	7
1 The Public Integrity System in the Brazilian Federal Executive Branch	9
Public integrity in Brazil: A snapshot	10
Addressing the mainstreaming challenge in the implementation of public integrity policies in Brazil	13
Streamline the promotion of public integrity in the Federal Executive Branch	18
References	23
Note	24
2 Strengthening the institutions of the Brazilian Public Integrity System (SIPEF)	25
Strengthening the Integrity Management Units	26
Enhancing CGU's role as the Central Body of the Public Integrity System in the Federal Executive	36
References	41

FIGURES

Figure 2.1. Relative amount of work of the UGI in the three competence areas in accordance with Ordinance 57/2019	26
Figure 2.2. Perceived challenges to an effective internal co-ordination on public integrity amongst selected UGI	28
Figure 2.3. Units designated as Integrity Managament Units in the Brazilian federal executive	34

TABLES

Table 1.1. Integrity Functions	10
Table 2.1. Responsibilities of CGU Departments for Integrity Promotion and Prevention of Corruption	37

Follow OECD Publications on:

http://twitter.com/OECD_Pubs

http://www.facebook.com/OECDPublications

http://www.linkedin.com/groups/OECD-Publications-4645871

http://www.youtube.com/oecdilibrary

http://www.oecd.org/oecddirect/

Executive summary

Mainstreaming integrity policies to ensure their effective implementation throughout the public administration is a challenge in all countries. Gaps are often observed between what legislation or policies on integrity stipulate and what is put into practice in public entities, hampering change in organisational cultures and the behaviour of public servants.

Integrity is the responsibility of all public servants. Nonetheless, dedicated integrity units can help overcome the challenge of mainstreaming integrity policies to promote organisational cultures of integrity. International experience shows the value of having such specialised and dedicated persons or units that are responsible and held accountable for the implementation and promotion of integrity laws and policies within their entities.

This report focuses on the challenge of mainstreaming integrity policies throughout the federal executive in Brazil. It reviews the current institutional arrangements and the ongoing efforts of the Office of the Comptroller General of the Union (CGU) to effectively implement integrity policies. Based on this review, the report provides recommendations to strengthen the integrity system in the federal executive branch.

Main findings

Recognising the challenge of mainstreaming integrity policies throughout its 186 federal entities, Brazil undertook two major initiatives over the past decades to reach out to the different organisational levels. First, in 2007, Brazil established the Ethics Management System of the Federal Executive Branch (SGEP). More recently, and based on the Integrity Programmes introduced by the CGU in 2017, Brazil established the Public Integrity System of the Federal Executive Branch (SIPEF).

However, the review has brought to light some challenges and areas for improvements.

- First, the co-existence of both the SGEP and the SIPEF with essentially the same goal creates complexity, opacity and overlapping responsibilities, especially for training and guidance on values, ethical dilemmas and conflict of interest situations. Indeed, the review found that the co-existence creates misunderstandings and confusion amongst public servants.
- Second, the members of the Ethics Commissions -- the sectorial units of the SGEP -- serve on a temporary basis, and often do not have time to develop specialised knowledge on integrity or establish trust-based relationships within their public entity. In addition, the Ethics Commissions can receive reports about potential integrity breaches and issue reprimands (*censura*). This mixing of prevention with enforcement-related tasks could create tensions with their role on providing guidance and overlap with the federal disciplinary regime.
- Finally, the SIPEF provides an opportunity for the CGU to review its Secretariat of Transparency and Corruption Prevention (STPC) to avoid overlaps and clarify responsibilities, Currently, similar to the overlap between the Federal Ethics Management System and the Public Integrity System, the responsibilities of the Directorate for Integrity Promotion (DPI) and the Directorate for the Prevention of Corruption (DPC) are blurred and partly overlapping, which leads to a lack of clarity, the risk of sending mixed messages, misunderstandings, and, therefore, potentially a waste of scarce resources.

Main recommendations

To address the challenges identified, the report provides a series of concrete recommendations to strengthen the promotion of integrity policies throughout the federal executive branch and help build open cultures of organisational integrity.

- The establishment of the SIPEF and the ongoing revision of the 1994 Code of Professional Ethics and the 2000 Code of Conduct for High Officials in the Federal Public Administration provide an opportunity to clarify concepts and streamline responsibilities for promoting cultures of organisational integrity in the federal executive branch. In particular, Brazil could consider moving the responsibility for supporting the management of public ethics and conflict of interest from the SGEP to the SIPEF and its institutions, thus leading to a single system that avoids overlaps and misunderstandings. Furthermore, Brazil could consider broadening the scope of the SIPEF to apply to the entire federal public administration.

- Within the SIPEF, the Integrity Management Units (UGI) are responsible for promoting guidance and training related to public integrity and for supporting integrity risk management. As such, the UGI could replace the current preventive tasks of the Ethics Commissions and become dedicated units with permanent and professionalised staff. This requires clarifying the existing normative framework and updating the guidance issued by the CGU. Furthermore, the CGU should continue the ongoing efforts to strengthen the institutional design and capacities of the UGI to fulfil their core mandate related to prevention, co-ordination, guidance and support on public integrity, including conflict of interest management, integrity risk management, and guidance on ethical dilemmas.

- The CGU, the central organ of the SIPEF, could strengthen the STPC by streamlining the tasks related to public integrity and the SIPEF under the responsibility of the DPI. In turn, the DPC could build on recent initiatives by promoting surveys and exploring the use of innovative tools, data and data analytics or undertaking research projects with academia. The CGU could consider strengthening the current DPC by building its capacities as a unit responsible for providing methodological and research advice to all units in the STPC. This internal rearrangement could help clarify responsibilities while fostering the development of specialised skills over time.

1 The Public Integrity System in the Brazilian Federal Executive Branch

Reflecting the federal nature and size of the country, the integrity system in Brazil is complex. Recognising this challenge, Brazil introduced the Ethics Management System of the Federal Executive Branch in 2007 and, in 2021, the Public Integrity System of the Federal Executive Branch (SIPEF). This chapter provides a snapshot of this system and focuses on the challenge of mainstreaming integrity policies throughout the federal executive branch. Brazil could improve significantly both clarity and coherence of the system by transferring the responsibilities for supporting the management of public ethics and conflict of interest to the SIPEF and its institutions. In turn, aspects related to enforcement should remain separated and the current institutional arrangement reviewed.

Public integrity in Brazil: A snapshot

The OECD defines public integrity as the consistent alignment of, and adherence to, shared ethical values, principles and norms for upholding and prioritising the public interest over private interests in the public sector (OECD, 2017[1]). An integrity system, whether at the government (national and sub-national) or organisational level, includes different actors with responsibilities for defining, supporting, controlling and enforcing public integrity. These include the "core" integrity actors, such as the institutions, units or individuals responsible for implementing integrity policies, but also "complementary" integrity actors with key support functions such as finance, human resource management and public procurement (OECD, 2020[2]; OECD, 2017[1]).

For both the core and complementary integrity actors, there are a number of integrity functions, as laid out in Table 1.1. The assignment of responsibilities related to public integrity depend on the institutional and jurisdictional setup of a country. For example, some countries give core responsibilities for integrity with a central government body or other key ministry, whereas others will make this the responsibility of an independent or autonomous body. Typically, complementary integrity functions are assigned to the institutions responsible for education, industry, civil society and human resource management, as well as supreme audit institutions, regulatory agencies, and electoral bodies.

Table 1.1. Integrity Functions

SYSTEM	CULTURE	ACCOUNTABILITY
<ul><li>Assigning clear responsibilities</li><li>Ensuring mechanisms to support horizontal and vertical co-operation</li><li>Designing and implementing the integrity strategy or strategies</li><li>Monitoring and evaluating the integrity strategy or strategies</li><li>Setting integrity standards</li></ul>	<ul><li>Integrating integrity into human resource management (e.g. assessing the fairness of reward and promotion systems) and personnel management (e.g. integrity as criterion for selection, evaluation and career promotion)</li><li>Building capacity and raising the awareness of public officials</li><li>Providing advice and counselling</li><li>Implementing measures to cultivate openness</li><li>Opening channels and implementing mechanisms for complaints and whistle-blower protection</li><li>Raising awareness in society</li><li>Conducting civic education programmes</li><li>Implementing measures to support integrity in companies</li><li>Implementing measures to support integrity in civil society organisations</li></ul>	<ul><li>Assessing and managing integrity risks</li><li>Applying internal audit</li><li>Implementing enforcement mechanisms</li><li>Applying independent oversight and audit</li><li>Applying access to information and implementing open government measures</li><li>Engaging stakeholders across the policy cycle</li><li>Preventing and managing conflict of interest</li><li>Implementing integrity measures for lobbying</li><li>Implementing integrity measures in financing of political parties and election campaigns</li></ul>

Source: (OECD, 2020[2])

In Brazil, there are several integrity actors, co-ordination mechanisms and a variety of relevant legislation and policies that cover the different functions of an integrity system as outlined in Table 1.1. Box 1.1 provides a concise overview, focusing only on the most relevant elements. Additional complexity arises, as Brazil is a federal republic as well as a large and heterogeneous country. The federal system includes 26 states, a Federal District and over 5 000 different municipalities. Each level is autonomous in legislating and providing services, as long as these do not conflict with the powers exclusively provided or legislated by the Federal Union. Brazil is also one of the world's most populous countries with over 200 million inhabitants, the fifth largest country in the world with a territory almost as big as Europe, as well as one of the largest global economies.

Box 1.1. Main integrity actors, co-ordination mechanisms and regulations at federal level in Brazil

Main integrity actors in Brazil

At the federal level, Brazil's integrity system has several "core" and "complementary" integrity actors.

- The Office of the Comptroller General of the Union (*Controladoria-Geral da União*, CGU) is in charge of internal control and audit, disciplinary enforcement, promoting integrity and transparency in the public sector and the whole of society, negotiating and monitoring leniency agreements and has ombudsman functions. It is the central body of the recently established the Public Integrity System of the Federal Executive Branch (*Sistema de Integridade Pública do Poder Executivo Federal*, SIPEF).
- The Public Ethics Commission (*Comissão de Ética Pública*, CEP) currently ensures compliance with the Code of Conduct of the Federal High Administration and the Conflict-of-Interest Law. It coordinates and supervises the Ethics Management System.
- The Federal Court of Accounts (*Tribunal de Contas da União*, TCU) is the Supreme Audit Institution of Brazil and plays a vital role in ensuring oversight, foresight and insights for public policies, including integrity policies.
- The Federal Office of the Public Prosecutor (*Ministério Público da União*) has the responsibility to protect legality, the public interest and the participation in criminal procedures, including those related to corruption offenses.
- The Federal Police of Brazil (*Polícia Federal do Brasil*) is authorized and empowered to investigate corruption cases that involve federal funds or federal entities. For this purpose, specialized anti-corruption units have been deployed across the country.
- The Office of the Attorney General of the Union (*Advocacia-Geral da União*, AGU) provides legal advice to the President regarding the legality of administrative acts and acts as a federal government representative in legal disputes before the court.
- Finally, the Financial Intelligence Unit (*Conselho de Controle das Atividades Financeiras*, COAF) is competent to receive, examine and identify suspicious cases of illicit activities provided for in Law and is the central agency for the prevention of money laundering and the financing of terrorism.

Main co-ordination mechanisms relevant for integrity at federal level in Brazil

Brazil's National Strategy against Corruption and Money Laundering (*Estratégia Nacional de Combate à Corrupção e à Lavagem de Dinheiro*, ENCCLA) is the national policy co-ordination mechanism on integrity, anti-corruption and anti-money-laundering. It brings together almost 90 actors from the three branches and civil society to facilitate the exchange of good practices and the development and implementation of joint activities.

The Anticorruption Inter-ministerial Committee (*Comitê Interministerial de Combate à Corrupção*, CICC), established by Decree 9755/2019, advises the Presidency on formulating, implementing, and evaluating integrity and anti-corruption policies. In December of 2020, the Committee adopted the Anti-corruption Plan 2020-2025 for the Federal Branch to structure and implement actions to improve the mechanisms for prevention, detection, and sanctioning of corruption. The CICC is co-ordinated by the CGU, and currently integrated by the heads of the Ministry of Justice, the Ministry of the Economy, the Institutional Security Office, the Attorney General of the Union and the Central Bank of Brazil. A technical body assists the CICC and working groups to analyse specific issues can be formed.

> In turn, the Council for Public Transparency and Fight against Corruption (*Conselho de Transparência Pública e Combate à Corrupção*, CTPCC), established through Decree 9468/2018 (updated by Decree 9986/2019) and led by the CGU, formulates guidelines and proposals on transparency, open government and access to public information, among other activities. It is currently integrated by several actors from the federal executive as well as civil society organisations. The CTPCC is also discussed in the forthcoming OECD Open Government Review (OECD, forthcoming[3]).
>
> **Main regulations on public integrity at federal level in Brazil**
>
> Brazil has several regulations that together build the country's legal framework for public integrity.
>
> - Decree 10756/2021 established the Public Integrity System of the Federal Executive Branch (SIPEF) and is the legal base for mainstreaming integrity policies throughout federal entities.
> - The Code of Professional Ethics of the Public Servant of the Federal Executive Branch (Decree 1171/1994) defines deontological rules, duties, and prohibitions for public officials.
> - Law 8112/1990 regulates the civil service regime for all public officials. The Law includes a list of duties and prohibitions. In case of infringements, public officials will be subject to a disciplinary procedure defined by the law.
> - Law 12846/2013, known as the Anti-corruption Law or the Clean Company Law, specifies civil and administrative legal obligations for wrongful acts committed by Brazilian officials against national or foreign public administration executed for their personal benefit.
> - Law 12813/2013 defines Brazil's legal and policy framework concerning conflict of interests in the federal executive.
>
> Source: Based on OECD fact finding and (OECD, 2012[4]).

As outlined in the OECD Recommendation on Public Integrity, the variety of actors require establishing clear responsibilities and mechanisms for co-operation. The responsibilities at the relevant levels (organisational, subnational and national) for designing, leading and implementing the elements of an integrity system need to be clear. In addition, mechanisms to promote horizontal and vertical co-operation between the integrity actors and where possible, with and between subnational levels of government, support coherence and avoid overlap and gaps within the system (OECD, 2017[1]). For Brazil, these arrangements and challenges will be analysed in a forthcoming OECD Integrity Review (OECD, forthcoming[5]), which will build upon previous OECD work with Brazil (OECD, 2012[4]; OECD, 2017[6]; OECD, 2013[7]; OECD, 2020[8]).

This report contributes to this analysis by focusing on the specific challenge of mainstreaming integrity policies throughout the federal executive in Brazil. In line with the OECD Recommendation on Public Integrity, this mainstreaming should go beyond a formal compliance with the existing regulations but achieve real change in behaviours (Rangone, 2021[9]). In many countries, gaps often exist between what the legislation or policies stipulate and what is put into practice in the day-to-day work of a public entity. In particular, the challenge involves translating and anchoring standards into organisational realities to achieve effective changes in organisational cultures and the behaviour of public servants. This report reviews the ongoing efforts of the Office of the Comptroller General of the Union (*Controladoria Geral da União*, CGU) to mainstream public integrity policies across the Federal public administration and provides concrete recommendations for managing integrity risks and promoting cultures of organisational public integrity (OECD, forthcoming[10]).

Addressing the mainstreaming challenge in the implementation of public integrity policies in Brazil

Integrity is the responsibility of all public servants. In particular, integrity leadership at all levels is essential to demonstrate a public sector organisation's commitment to integrity; with their function of being ethical leaders and providing an example, they play a crucial part in the effective promotion of an integrity culture (OECD, 2017[1]; OECD, 2009[11]; OECD, 2020[2]; OECD, forthcoming[12]). For example, in Colombia, the Integrated Planning and Management Model (*Modelo Integrado de Planeación y Gestión*, MIPG) requires managers to periodically report on their actions related to integrity, transparency and other cross-cutting issues (Función Pública, 2017[13]). In France, senior management are personally responsible and ultimately accountable for the effective implementation and promotion of an organisation's integrity programme (Agence Française Anticorruption, 2020[14]).

Nonetheless, dedicated "integrity actors" in public entities can contribute to overcome the challenge of mainstreaming integrity policies to ensure implementation in public entities and to promote organisational cultures of integrity. International experience shows the value of having a specialised and dedicated person or unit that is responsible and held accountable for the internal implementation and promotion of integrity laws and policies (OECD, 2009[11]; G20, 2017[15]; OECD, 2019[16]).

Recognising this challenge, Brazil undertook two major initiatives over the past decades:

- In 2007, the Ethics Management System of the Federal Executive Branch (*Sistema de Gestão da Ética do Poder Executivo federal*, SGEP) has been established through Decree 6029/2007.
- In 2021, the Public Integrity System of the Federal Executive Branch (*Sistema de Integridade Pública do Poder Executivo Federal*, SIPEF) has been established through Decree 10756/2021.

While the Ethics Management System applies to the whole of the Federal executive branch, including the entities of the indirect administration, the SIPEF currently covers bodies and entities of the direct, autarchic and foundational administration (*administração direta, autárquica e fundacional*) (Box 1.2).

Box 1.2. The Brazilian Federal Executive Branch

The Federal Administration is composed of the Direct Administration and the Indirect Administration.

The Direct Administration consists of services integrated into the administrative structure of the Presidency of the Republic and the Ministries. The Presidency of the Republic is the supreme body and independent representative of the Executive Power of the Union, encompassing all higher administrative activities at the federal level, in politics, planning, co-ordination and control of the country's socio-economic development and national security. In turn, the Ministries are autonomous bodies at the top of the Federal Administration, located just below the Presidency of the Republic.

The Indirect Administration comprises entities of the Federal Executive Power endowed with legal personality and their own assets and with administrative and financial autonomy (*autarquias*), public foundations, mixed capital companies and State Owned Enterprises.

Source: Information provided by the Office of the Comptroller General, Law 9784/1999

The Ethics Management System established responsibilities to mainstream public ethics and manage conflict of interest in the Federal executive

In 1994, Brazil introduced the Code of Professional Ethics of the Public Servant of the Federal Executive Branch (*Código de Ética Profissional do Servidor Público Civil do Poder Executivo federal*, Decree 1171/1994). The Code requires establishing Ethics Commission (*Comissões de Ética*) in every entity of the Federal executive to support its mainstreaming and implementation. Each Ethics Commission has three sitting members and three alternates, chosen from among public servants of its permanent staff and appointed by the highest officer of the respective entity or body for non-coinciding terms of three years. The Ethics Commissions are required to have an Executive Secretariat headed by a civil servant or employee of the permanent staff of the entity, occupying a management position compatible with its structure, the technical and material support necessary to comply with its attributions (Decree 6029/2007).

The Ethics Commissions are responsible to guide and advise public officials on professional ethics, to build awareness of consequences of ethical breaches and to receive notice of possible breaches. They provide information to the human resources department about the ethical record of public officials through their career development and can issue a reprimand (*censura*) in case of breaches to the Code.

In 2007, the Ethics Commissions were incorporated into the Ethics Management System of the Federal Executive Branch (Decree 6029/2007), which has the following objectives:

- linking the agencies, programmes and actions related to public ethics
- contributing to the implementation of public policies using transparency and access to information as fundamental instruments for the exercise of public ethics management (see also the Open Government Review of Brazil (OECD, forthcoming[3]))
- promoting compatibility and coherence of standards, technical and management procedures related to public ethics
- developing actions to establish and implement procedures to encourage and enhance institutional performance in the management of public ethics in the Brazilian government.

A recent evaluation of the SGEP, carried out amongst other through the application of the Ethics Management Evaluation Questionnaire in June-July 2020 to which 117 Commissions responded, evidenced that 88% of the Commissions have an Executive Secretary in place. Of these, 29% have exclusive dedication, 31% hold a managerial position, 62% are having their own space and 58% have established a work plan (Comissão de Ética Pública, 2021[17]). These results show that while the SGEP advanced in its implementation, it still faces challenges, especially outside of the state owned enterprises. Interviews carried out for this OECD report underscored that often a main weakness is a lack of support by the highest authorities.

In turn, the Public Ethics Commission (Comissão de Ética Pública, CEP, Box 1.3), established in 1999, coordinates, evaluates and supervises the Ethics Management System. Since 2000, the CEP has been responsible for implementing and enforcing the Code of Conduct of the High Federal Administration and providing advice on conflict of interest. In addition, the CEP monitors and conducts an annual evaluation of the implementation of ethics management system in the Federal Executive Branch. The CEP can conduct technical visits, which are on-site initiatives to disseminate and assess the progress in adopting actions to establish a more effective ethics infrastructure. Furthermore, the CEP has been promoting and providing various training courses, including the Course on Management and Investigation of Public Ethics and the International Seminar on Ethics in Management, for example.

> **Box 1.3. The Public Ethics Commission**
>
> In 1999, Brazil established the Public Ethics Commission (*Comissão de Ética Pública*, CEP) as an advisory body to the President of the Republic and the Ministers of State on matters of public ethics. The CEP is composed of seven members appointed by the President of the Republic for a staggered term of three years, with the possibility of extension for one additional term of three years.
>
> Over the years, the CEP's role has evolved. At the beginning, its activities were restricted to consulting the President on matters of an ethical nature. Later, with the approval of the Code of Conduct of the High Federal Administration in 2000, it became responsible for implementing and monitoring the Code. An Executive Secretariat provides technical and administrative support.
>
> The CEP submits to the President of the Republic measures to improve ethics management, resolves doubts on interpreting its norms, deliberates on omissions and decides on cases not covered by the Code of Professional Ethics (Decree 171/1994). Since 2007, the CEP also co-ordinates, evaluates and supervises the Public Ethics Management System of the Federal Executive (*Sistema de Gestão da Ética do Poder Executivo federal*, SGEP, Decree 6029/2007). The CEP approves the internal regulation of the SGEP and chooses its President. Over the years, the CEP has been promoting actions aimed at ensuring the adequacy and effectiveness of ethical standards in the Federal executive, organising training for public officials and civil society.
>
> Source: Prepared by the OECD based on Decree 171/1994, Decree 6029/2007. See also (OECD, 2012[4])

A second key element of the normative framework on public integrity is Law 12813/2013 on managing conflict of interest in the federal executive branch. The Law applies to all public officials within the federal executive. However, its scope is currently limited to the divulgation or use of privileged information and to pursuing private external activities that are incompatible with the current public position and functions. Nonetheless, the use of privileged information has not been regulated yet for public servants that do not belong to the higher administration as defined in the Law. A preliminary analysis indicates that the conflict-of-interest framework could be improved taking into account the standards of the OECD (2004[18]). The forthcoming OECD Integrity Review will review this aspect in depth (OECD, forthcoming[5]).

Furthermore, under the current framework, the competence to provide guidance and opinions in case of doubts concerning (potential) exercise of private activity that is not expressly prohibited, as well as to supervise and formally assess conflict of interest situations, has been divided between the CEP and the CGU. Currently, the CEP is responsible for public officials belonging to the high administration and the CGU for all other public servants.

The Public Integrity System is an important step towards strengthening integrity policies and ensuring their mainstreaming in the Federal Executive

The CGU is the internal control body of the Federal Government and, since its creation in 2001, has been a core element of the federal government's strategy to enhance integrity and prevent corruption in Brazil (OECD, 2012[4]). The CGU has responsibilities in a number of core and complementary integrity functions, as outlined in Table 1.1, such as promoting public integrity, contributing to the framework for managing conflict of interest, preventing and fighting corruption, supporting integrity risk management, internal control and audit, disciplinary enforcement as well as ombudsman functions, promoting social control and transparency.

In particular, the CGU is responsible for leading the mandatory Integrity Programmes to prevent, detect, punish and remediate corruption, fraud, illicit acts and violations of the standards of ethics and conduct in all public entities of the Federal Executive. Decree 9203/2017 introduced the Integrity Programmes that were subsequently regulated through Ordinance 1089/2018 and Ordinance 57/2019. Integrity Programmes have to be developed along the following axes:

- Commitment and support from senior management.
- Existence of a unit responsible for implementation in the organ or entity.
- Analysis, evaluation and management of risks associated with integrity.
- Monitoring of the elements of the Integrity Programme.

Integrity Programmes aim to ensure that internal units responsible for integrity-related activities and areas such as corruption prevention, internal audit, disciplinary enforcement and transparency work together in co-ordination to ensure integrity and minimise integrity risks. As such, the Integrity Programmes focus on prevention and aim at reducing integrity risks in public entities. Developing an Integrity Programme implies going beyond ensuring formal compliance with Laws and regulations and should aim at promoting cultures of integrity within the public entities.

The CGU established procedures for developing, implementing and monitoring these Integrity Programmes, such as the 2017 *Manual for the Implementation of Integrity Programmes* or the 2018 *Practical Guide for Implementing a Programme of Integrity*. Currently, the CGU is carrying out an evaluation of the Integrity Programmes. Some preliminary results have informed the findings of the report through the discussions with CGU staff.

The first mandatory step of an Integrity Programme is establishing an Integrity Management Unit (*Unidade de Gestão da Integridade*, UGI) within the public entity. The UGI coordinates the development of the internal Integrity Plan of the public entity, as well as its subsequent implementation, monitoring and evaluation. These Integrity Plans need to be approved by senior management and set out the integrity measures and an action plan for their implementation.

Key elements required in the integrity plans include (Ordinance 57/2019):

- a description of the body or entity
- establishment of the integrity units
- assessment of the integrity risks and measures to address them
- provisions for monitoring and the periodic updating integrity plans.

Since 2017, the CGU has supported the establishment of UGIs and the elaboration of integrity plans in all 186 entities of the Federal Executive government. The recent Public Integrity System of the Federal Executive Branch (SIPEF), established in July 2021, further formalises and strengthens the normative basis for the Integrity Programmes and the UGI and therefore for promoting integrity throughout the Brazilian Federal Executive. The SIPEF establishes the UGI as the systems' responsible sectorial units, expanding their functions and responsibilities (Box 1.4). These responsibilities could be summarised as articulating different integrity efforts within the entity, but also include providing guidance, training and support on matters related to public integrity and integrity risk management.

> **Box 1.4. Functions of the UGI within the Public Integrity System of the Federal Executive Branch (SIPEF)**
>
> According to Decree 10756/2021, which established the SIPEF, the UGI functions include:
>
> - advise the highest authority of the body or entity on matters related to the integrity program
> - liaise with the other units of the agency or entity that perform integrity functions to obtain the information necessary for monitoring the integrity programme
> - coordinate the structuring, execution and monitoring of its integrity programme
> - promote guidance and training, within the body or entity, on matters relating to the integrity programme
> - prepare and periodically review the integrity plan
> - coordinate the management of risks to integrity
> - monitor and evaluate, within the scope of the body or entity, the implementation of the measures established in the integrity plan
> - propose actions and measures, within the scope of the body or entity, based on information and data related to the management of the integrity program
> - evaluate the actions and measures related to the integrity program suggested by the other units of the body or entity
> - report to the highest authority of the body or entity on the progress of the integrity program
> - participate in activities that require the execution of joint actions by the units that are part of SIPEF, with a view to improving the exercise of common activities
> - report to the central body the situations that compromise the integrity program and adopt the necessary measures for its remediation
> - perform other activities of the integrity programs provided for in art. 19 of Decree 9203/2017.
>
> Source: Decree 10756/2021.

As mentioned above, the CGU has a shared responsibility in the management of conflict of interest. Indeed, to facilitate the management of conflict of interests, public servants can send to the human resources unit of their entities a request for consultation on possible conflict of interest situations. In case the public entity concludes that there is a potential conflict of interest situation, the consultation is automatically forwarded to the CGU. These consultations are submitted through the Electronic System for Conflict of Interest Prevention (*Sistema Eletrônico de Prevenção de Conflito de Interesses*, SeCI, Box 1.5).

> **Box 1.5. Conflict of Interest Law and Electronic System for Prevention of Conflict of Interest**
>
> Focusing on the preventive approach of Law 12813/2013 and with the aim to facilitate interaction with the public employee, the CGU has developed the Electronic System for Prevention of Conflict of Interest (*Sistema Eletrônico de Prevenção de Conflito de Interesses*, SeCI). The electronic system allows federal public servants or employees to submit formal consultations to find out if they are likely to fall within a situation of conflict of interest, or to request authorisation to exercise private activity. It also enables the applicant to monitor its consultation and lodge appeals.
>
> Between 10 July 2014 and 27 March 2020, federal public officials submitted 7961 consultations on conflict of interest to their agencies and entities through the SeCI. Out of the 7207 consultations analysed, 916 involved a relevant conflict of interest risk and were submitted to the CGU for further analysis. The CGU confirmed the existence of a relevant conflict of interest risk in 279 cases, advising against the exercise of the private activity under analysis. In relation to 198 consultations, CGU considered that the identified risk of conflict of interest could be mitigated provided the interested party agreed to comply with certain conditions. In another 118 consultations, CGU did not identify any relevant risk of conflict of interest, authorising the interested party to exercise the activity under consideration.
>
> Source: (UNDOC, 2018[19]); (CGU, n.d.[20])

Streamline the promotion of public integrity in the Federal Executive Branch

Brazil could transfer the responsibilities for supporting the management of public ethics and conflict of interest to the SIPEF and its institutions to enhance clarity and coherence of its framework

Both the Ethics Management and more recently the Public Integrity System are responses to the mainstreaming challenge. Nonetheless, the fact-finding of the OECD, that involved a survey, interviews and focus group discussions as well as an in-depth review of the relevant Brazilian legislation and policy documents, evidenced some challenges related to the design and implementation as well as overlaps or unclear responsibilities in particular in relation to the promotion of public integrity cultures and managing integrity risks. As mentioned above, while public integrity has many elements and typically involve different actors and units, there also needs to be coherence and clarity with respect to the promotion of integrity at entity level to avoid potential mixed messages or confusion amongst public servants.

While the conceptual debate is complex, both "ethics' and "integrity" are aiming at promoting high standards of behaviour of public servants. In fact, the OECD uses "ethics management" and "integrity management" as synonyms. While earlier OECD publications refer to "ethics", recent publications prefer the term "integrity", indicating a shift to modern styles of integrity management that combine rules-based with values-based approaches (OECD, 2009[11]). In fact, the 2017 OECD Recommendation on Public Integrity has been the result of a process reviewing the 1998 Recommendation of the OECD Council on Improving Ethical Conduct in the Public Service, which by then provided for the first time guidance to policy makers on the management of ethics in the public sector. The Recommendation on Public Integrity incorporates this perspective by calling adherents to set high standards of conduct for public officials, while opening the scope to provide policy makers with a vision for a context dependent, behavioural, risk-based approach to public integrity that emphasises the relevance of cultivating culture of integrity across the whole of society (OECD, 2017[1]).

In the end, what matters more than the term is the definition of the concept, its operationalisation and ability to achieve impact in terms of behavioural change. Integrity – or ethics – management aim to promote integrity and prevent integrity violations (OECD, 2009[11]). Public integrity ensures a consistent alignment of, and adherence to, shared ethical values, principles and norms for upholding and prioritising the public interest over private interests in the public sector (OECD, 2017[1]). However, the co-existence of two systems in Brazil with essentially the same goal implies complexity and opacity, comes with a serious risk of overlaps, sending mixed messages and a lack of clarity with respect to responsibilities, especially regarding trainings and guidance on values, ethical dilemmas and conflict of interest situations. Indeed, the fact-finding evidenced that that the co-existence of an ethics system and the integrity programmes (and now the SIPEF) comes along with some misunderstandings and confusion amongst public servants.

Brazil could therefore clarify and streamline the responsibility and the concepts aimed at promoting cultures of organisational integrity in the Federal Executive by moving the responsibilities for supporting the management of public ethics and the managing conflict of interest from the ethics management system to the SIPEF and its institutions. This reform could provide the opportunity to broaden the scope of application of the SIPEF to the whole federal executive administration (Box 1.2). In turn, in close co-ordination with the SIPEF, the CEP could be maintained as an advisory body to the President of the Republic and to the Ministers of State and to oversee and promote the application of the current Code of Conduct of the High Federal Administration. By the time of the drafting of this report, an inter-institutional working group has been working on revising both the Code of Professional Ethics and the Code of Conduct of the High Federal Administration. This ongoing revision provides an opportunity to further clarify and streamline the guidance provided to public servants (see Chapter 2).

The OECD Recommendation on Regulatory Policy and Governance emphasises that governments should ensure that regulations are comprehensible and clear and should identify and reform overlapping regulations (OECD, 2012[21]). In addition, as emphasised in the OECD report on Applying Behavioural Insights to Public Integrity, the clarification of responsibilities across the public sector not only increases the effectiveness of an integrity system, but can also strengthen the integrity of individual decision makers (OECD, 2018[22]). Indeed, behavioural insights associated with simplification, convenience and salience, would suggest that many existing regulations may themselves be too complex and cumbersome to be effective (Lunn, 2014[23]). By streamlining the integrity and ethics systems as recommended, Brazil could simplify the presentation of what matters to promote a culture of integrity and limit the number or complexity of concepts associated with it. This streamlining will also help to promote the salience of the concept of public integrity. Evidence suggests that as human beings, public servants can pay attention to a limited number of attributes associated with any given option in front of them (Lunn, 2014[23]). Making the concept of integrity salient will facilitate communication on integrity-related matters and provide clarity with respect to key elements of integrity policies such as managing conflicts of interest, promoting open cultures of organisational integrity, integrity risk management or dealing with ethical dilemmas, i.e. dilemmas arising due to legal grey areas and/or conflicting values (Chapter 2).

Finally, Brazil should consider reviewing the coherence and alignment of the new SIPEF in terms of connections and concepts with the following federal systems that are related to public integrity (see also forthcoming Integrity Review of Brazil (OECD, forthcoming[5])):

- the Internal Control System of the Federal Executive Branch (*Sistema de Controle Interno do Poder Executivo Federal*, SCI) to align concepts related to risk management, internal control and audit
- the Administrative Disciplinary System of the Federal Executive Branch (*Sistema de Correição do Poder Executivo Federal*, SISCOR) to ensure the enforcement of integrity breaches
- the Ombdusman System of the Federal Executive Branch (*Sistema de Ouvidoria do Poder Executivo Federal*) for aspects related to consulting and receiving reports and feed-back from citizens and users of public services in relation to public integrity (for an in-depth analysis on the shortcomings of the current system, see the OECD Open Government Review (OECD, forthcoming[3])).

Supporting public ethics and providing guidance on managing conflict of interest are best provided by dedicated units

As described above, the Ethics Commissions are currently responsible at the level of public entities for guiding and raising awareness on public ethics as well as for receiving notice of possible breaches of the Code of Professional Ethics.

However, the Ethics Commissions in Brazil suffer from similar weaknesses as identified in other countries with comparable arrangements (OECD, 2017[24]; OECD, 2021[25]; OECD, 2019[26]):

- First, the organisation as a commission comes along with inherent challenges. The members of the Ethics Commissions are selected among the staff from the federal entity on a temporary basis, often do not have any previous experience in the subject matter and require specialised training to fulfil effectively their tasks. In Brazil, the CEP provides such trainings. However, given that members are selected for three, maximum six years, it is difficult to establish experience, which affects learning, continuity and effectiveness of the Ethics Commissions. The rotation makes it also difficult to establish a "visible" face for integrity in the public entity and could undermine the establishment of trust that is required to fulfil credibly the function of advising on often sensitive issues. Furthermore, given that being a member of the Commission is an additional task without additional remuneration, the work on promoting ethics will often be only the second priority or depend strongly on the motivation of the selected individuals.

- Second, the fact that the Ethics Commissions in Brazil can receive reports about potential breaches and issue reprimands (*censura*) is mixing prevention with enforcement related tasks. This does not make them the best place to provide public officials a safe place where they can seek guidance about ethical dilemmas or situations where they may have committed an error (OECD, 2018[22]). The unit or person in charge of providing advice should not be involved in any tasks related to investigation or sanctioning of integrity breaches, but rather be a safe haven where employees can speak up and ask questions without fearing direct repercussions. Moreover, confidentiality of the questions as well as the advice provided should be ensured to promote a trustworthy environment.

In turn, within the SIPEF, the UGI are responsible for promoting guidance and training on matters relating to the Integrity Programme and for supporting integrity risk management. With support from CGU, the UGI already played a key role in the process of identifying the new Values of the Federal Public Service and in promoting the campaign #IntegridadeSomosTodosNós. As such, the UGI are well placed to use the Values as an entry point to mainstream integrity into processes and day-to-day practice relevant in the context of their public entity and promote an open organisational culture of integrity (see Chapter 2).

As mentioned, the co-existence of the Ethics Commissions and the UGI, however, creates confusion amongst public servants. In line with the previous recommendation, Brazil could therefore consider transferring the preventive functions related to ethics and conflict-of-interest management from the Ethics Commissions to the UGI. From another perspective, this could be equivalent to transforming the Executive Secretariats of the Ethics Commissions into UGI with permanent and professionalised staff under the SIPEF, as has been recommended for the similar case of the federal level in Mexico (OECD, 2017[24]; OECD, 2019[26]).

However, while the UGI have the potential to become dedicated units with permanent and professionalised staff under the SIPEF, the current normative framework does not require this.[1] The fact finding in the context of this project found that this comes along with challenges and weaknesses in delivering the mandate and functions of the UGI (Chapter 2). Box 1.6 provides some general arguments in favour of such a dedicated space for integrity in an organisation. Brazil could thus focus on strengthening the UGI by requiring them to be a dedicated unit and by aligning their organisational design with their mandate. Then, the role of the UGI within the SIPEF could be communicated clearly and it would be easier to invest into the required capacities and skills to co-ordinate, plan and monitor the Integrity Plans and provide support and guidance on ethical dilemmas, potential conflict of interests, integrity risk management and other questions related to public integrity. This would address the identified weaknesses, give public integrity a visible and dedicated place within the organisation, and contribute to improve both clarity and conceptual coherence of the institutional framework and entity level. Chapter 2 provides further recommendations on how to strengthen the UGI along these lines.

Box 1.6. A dedicated place for integrity at organisational levels

There are several reasons why it is important to have a unit dedicated to integrity in an organisation:

- A visible place for integrity management in the organisational structure increases the scope of coordination between integrity management instruments and, therefore, allows synergies between instruments. The explicit designation of this coordination function to a person, group or organisational unit will significantly increase the possibility of producing said coordination.

- A clear location of integrity management in the organisational structure also allows a true accumulation of expertise, as recommendations, insights and good practices would be complied in a single area within the organisation.

- The anchoring of the integrity management system in the organisation also guarantees the continuity of integrity policies. In practice, it is common that, even when integrity management draws attention and enthusiasm when launched for the first time, this tends to decrease after some time. Holding a person or entity accountable for long-term integrity management and asking them to report on their progress will significantly reduce this risk.

- The organisational anchoring also has a symbolic element. It sends the signal that integrity is deemed important within the organisation. A typical rule in the theory of organisational design is that "the structure follows the strategy": the structure reflects the areas of strategic importance for the organisation. If an organisation seeks to attribute importance to integrity, this shall be reflected in its organisational chart.

- Providing integrity with its own position in the organisational chart also provides its own identity. A separate identity does not mean that integrity management instruments are to be isolated from other relevant management areas, such as human resources or financial management. Neither does this mean that those responsible for integrity management have to try to take over areas or instruments of other areas that may be considered as integrity management instruments within their own competence sphere. Consequently, the cooperation and articulation among those responsible for integrity and actors of other areas is fundamental.

Source: (OECD, 2009[11])

Functions related to the enforcement of the legal framework should not be transferred to the UGI and their institutional arrangement clarified

As already mentioned, the Ethics Commissions currently also receive complaints and reports concerning potential infractions against the Code of Professional Ethics, carry out preliminary fact-checking of complaints concerning and have the power to issue reprimands (*censura*) in case of breaches to the Code. These functions should not be transferred to the UGI to avoid mixing preventive functions with punitive elements; nonetheless, the UGI could articulate and assure the implementation of such elements related to detection and enforcement.

In fact, the legal framework regulating the civil service regime for all public officials in Brazil (Law 8112/1990) includes a list of duties and prohibitions, whose breach leads to disciplinary liability on top of the civil, criminal and administrative liability that may cumulatively apply. The CGU's General Inspectorate for Administrative Discipline (*Corregedoria-Geral da União*) and, at entity level, the Federal Inspectorates (*Corregedorias Federais*) are the institutions competent to deal with such internal disciplinary cases; although they do not exist yet in all federal entities. Established in 2001, the inspectorates conducts investigations, either ex officio or upon receipt of a credible report, of possible misconduct by federal public officials. As the central unit of the Administrative Disciplinary System of the Federal Executive Branch (SISCOR), it co-ordinates, evaluates and supervises the activities of inspectorates and disciplinary committees within federal public organisations. Recently, the CGU updated the Disciplinary Procedures Management System (e-PAD), which is an online system aimed at storing and making available information on the disciplinary procedures of the Federal Executive Branch.

While an in-depth review of Brazil's disciplinary regime is out of the scope of this report and will be carried out in the forthcoming OECD Integrity Review of Brazil, a preliminary analysis seems to indicate an overlap of the investigative and punitive function of the Ethics Commissions with Law 8112/1990 and the Federal Inspectorates. Depending on the degree of this potential overlap, and if the preventive functions are transferred to the UGI as recommended above, the Ethics Commissions would either cease to have any function or could maintained focusing only on their role to enforce the current Code of Professional Ethics. Nonetheless, this role need to ensure a close co-ordination with the Federal Inspectorates, articulated through the Integrity Programmes and the UGI.

References

Agence Française Anticorruption (2020), *The French Anti-Corruption Agency Guidelines*, Agence française Anticorruption (AFA), Paris, https://www.agence-francaise-anticorruption.gouv.fr/files/2021-03/French%20AC%20Agency%20Guidelines%20.pdf (accessed on 20 September 2021). [14]

CGU (n.d.), *Electronic System for Prevention of Conflict of Interest*, https://seci.cgu.gov.br/SeCI/Login/Externo.aspx?ReturnUrl=%2fSeCI (accessed on 5 March 2021). [20]

Comissão de Ética Pública (2021), "BOLETIM INFORMATIVO do Sistema de Gestão da Ética do Poder Executivo Federal" 39, https://www.gov.br/planalto/pt-br/assuntos/etica-publica/sistema-de-gestao-da-etica/boletim-informativo/boletins-informativos-2021/BoletimInformativo39Outubro2021.pdf (accessed on 15 November 2021). [17]

Función Pública (2017), *Modelo Integrado de Planeación y Gestión*, https://www.funcionpublica.gov.co/web/mipg (accessed on 20 September 2021). [13]

G20 (2017), *G20 High Level Principles on Organizing Against Corruption*, http://www.g20.utoronto.ca/2017/2017-g20-acwg-anti-corruption.html. [15]

Lunn, P. (2014), *Regulatory Policy and Behavioural Economics*, OECD Publishing, Paris, https://dx.doi.org/10.1787/9789264207851-en. [23]

OECD (2021), *OECD Integrity Review of the State of Mexico: Enabling a Culture of Integrity*, OECD Public Governance Reviews, OECD Publishing, Paris, https://dx.doi.org/10.1787/daee206e-en. [25]

OECD (2020), *Auditing Decentralised Policies in Brazil: Collaborative and Evidence-Based Approaches for Better Outcomes*, OECD Public Governance Reviews, OECD Publishing, Paris, https://dx.doi.org/10.1787/30023307-en. [8]

OECD (2020), *OECD Public Integrity Handbook*, OECD Publishing, Paris, https://dx.doi.org/10.1787/ac8ed8e8-en. [2]

OECD (2019), *Follow up report on the OECD Integrity Review of Mexico: Responding to citizens' expectations*, OECD, Paris, https://www.oecd.org/gov/ethics/follow-up-integrity-review-mexico.pdf (accessed on 19 August 2021). [26]

OECD (2019), *La Integridad Pública en América Latina y el Caribe 2018-2019: De Gobiernos reactivos a Estados proactivos*, OECD, Paris, https://www.oecd.org/gov/ethics/integridad-publica-en-america-latina-caribe-2018-2019.htm. [16]

OECD (2018), *Behavioural Insights for Public Integrity: Harnessing the Human Factor to Counter Corruption*, OECD Public Governance Reviews, OECD Publishing, Paris, https://dx.doi.org/10.1787/9789264297067-en. [22]

OECD (2017), *Brazil's Federal Court of Accounts: Insight and Foresight for Better Governance*, OECD Public Governance Reviews, OECD Publishing, Paris, https://dx.doi.org/10.1787/9789264279247-en. [6]

OECD (2017), *OECD Integrity Review of Mexico: Taking a Stronger Stance Against Corruption*, OECD Public Governance Reviews, OECD Publishing, Paris, https://dx.doi.org/10.1787/9789264273207-en. [24]

OECD (2017), *OECD Recommendation of the Council on Public Integrity*, OECD, Paris, http://www.oecd.org/gov/ethics/Recommendation-Public-Integrity.pdf. [1]

OECD (2013), *Brazil's Supreme Audit Institution: The Audit of the Consolidated Year-end Government Report*, OECD Public Governance Reviews, OECD Publishing, Paris, https://dx.doi.org/10.1787/9789264188112-en. [7]

OECD (2012), *OECD Integrity Review of Brazil: Managing Risks for a Cleaner Public Service*, OECD Public Governance Reviews, OECD Publishing, Paris, https://dx.doi.org/10.1787/9789264119321-en. [4]

OECD (2012), *Recommendation of the Council on Regulatory Policy and Governance*, OECD/LEGAL/0390, https://legalinstruments.oecd.org/en/instruments/OECD-LEGAL-0390. [21]

OECD (2009), *Towards a Sound Integrity Framework: Instruments, Processes, Structures and Conditions for Implementation (GOV/PGC/GF(2009)1)*, Organisation for Economic Co-operation and Development, Paris. [11]

OECD (2004), "OECD Guidelines for Managing Conflict of Interest in the Public Service", in *Managing Conflict of Interest in the Public Service: OECD Guidelines and Country Experiences*, OECD Publishing, Paris, https://dx.doi.org/10.1787/9789264104938-2-en. [18]

OECD (forthcoming), *Behavioural Insights for Public Integrity: Strengthening integrity leadership in Brazil's federal executive branch*, OECD Publishing, Paris. [12]

OECD (forthcoming), *Integrity Review of Brazil*, OECD Publishing, Paris. [5]

OECD (forthcoming), *Modernising Integrity Risk Management in Brazil*, OECD Publishing, Paris. [10]

OECD (forthcoming), *Open Government Review of Brazil*, OECD Publishing, Paris. [3]

Rangone, N. (2021), "Making Law Effective: Behavioural Insights into Compliance", *European Journal of Risk Regulation*, Vol. 9, pp. 483-501, http://dx.doi.org/10.1017/err.2018.51. [9]

UNDOC (2018), *Provision of Technical Assistance by G20 Anti-corruption Working Group Countries. Information Provided by Brazil.*, https://www.unodc.org/documents/corruption/G20TechnicalAssistance/PROVISION_OF_TECHNICAL_ASSISTANCE_BY_BRAZIL_on_G20_ACWG.pdf (accessed on 5 March 2021). [19]

Note

[1] Even though, in fact, the Ordinance 57/2019 talks about "constituting" UGI, which is ambiguous and could mean to "set up", to "establish" or to "create".

2 Strengthening the institutions of the Brazilian Public Integrity System (SIPEF)

The institutions of the Public Integrity System of the Federal Executive Branch (SIPEF) in Brazil are the Integrity Management Units (UGI) as the sectorial units, and the Office of the Comptroller General of the Union (CGU), as its central organ. This chapter reviews the current design and functions of the UGI. The UGI should focus on promoting open cultures of organisational integrity by co-ordinating, planning and monitoring the Integrity Plans, providing guidance and training to public servants on public integrity and supporting integrity risk management, including managing conflict of interest. To carry out these tasks, the organisational structure and capacities of the UGI should be aligned with their responsibilities. The chapter further recommends to clarify the division of labour within CGU's Secretariat of Transparency and Corruption Prevention and with respect to how the CGU can contribute to strengthening the SIPEF by providing support, guidance and facilitating exchanges between public entities.

Strengthening the Integrity Management Units

To enhance the impact of the UGI, they should focus on preventive measures and promoting an open culture of organisational integrity

Chapter 1 emphasises the central role of the Integrity Management Units (*Unidade de Gestão da Integridade*, UGI) in the new Public Integrity System (SIPEF) and their potential to contribute to overcome the mainstreaming challenge in the federal executive. The UGI can be become the visible and pivotal area responsible for preventing corruption, fraud and other integrity violations and for promoting cultures of public integrity in their organisations.

Currently, Ordinance 57/2019 are mentioning three responsibilities of the UGI:

- Co-ordinate the structuring, implementation and monitoring of the Integrity Programmes.
- Provide guidance and training to public servants in areas related to the Integrity Programmes.
- Promote, together with other units of the public entity, other actions related to the implementation of the Integrity Programmes.

Today, all 186 public entities of the federal executive have designated an UGI and the monitoring portal from the CGU indicates that they are active, even though this data does not allow drawing conclusions concerning the quality of the implementation. For instance, 166 UGI have realised an assessment of integrity risks, all 186 UGI have approved an Integrity Plan and 159 UGI have established internal procedures for analysing consultations submitted by public servants concerning potential conflict-of-interest situations (Data from paineis.cgu.gov.br/integridadepublica).

The OECD Survey carried out in 2020 for this project shows that in this early stage of their existence, the UGI were focusing their time and resources mainly on their co-ordination function and the elaboration of the Integrity Programmes (Figure 2.1). Only a few UGI provided guidance or trainings and "other actions". These "other actions consist, for example, in communicating on public integrity or ensuring the involvement of and reporting to the highest authorities of the public entity (CGU, 2018[1]).

Figure 2.1. Relative amount of work of the UGI in the three competence areas in accordance with Ordinance 57/2019

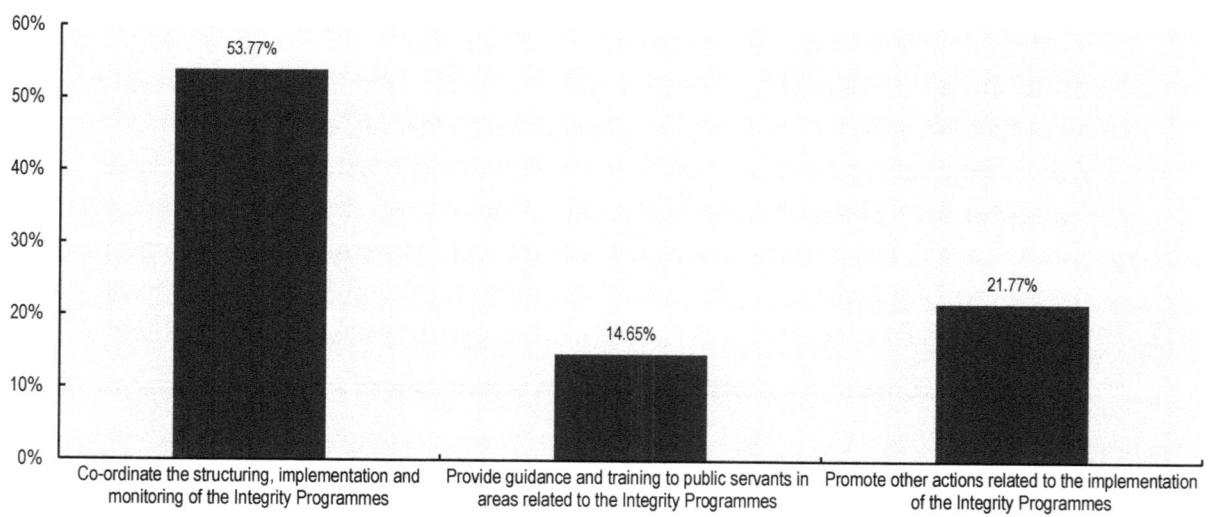

Note: The OECD questionnaire was sent to 35 UGI, from which 30 responses were received. For this Figure, 26 answers could be used. The sample is thus not representative but indicative and has been supported by qualitative interviews and a focus group.
Source: OECD Survey 2020

The three areas of Ordinance 57/2019, and in particular the first two, are certainly core competences of the UGI, and should be maintained. Nonetheless, the CGU could consider using the opportunity provided by the recent SIPEF to revise and fine-tune the guidance provided to the UGI and focus the mandate of these units on promoting an open culture of organisational integrity in line with the OECD Recommendation of Public Integrity (OECD, 2017[2]; OECD, 2020[3]). The UGI have a key role in promoting Integrity Programmes that are context dependent, i.e. reflecting the specificities of the respective public entity, behavioural, i.e. aimed at achieving actual change, and risk-based.

Following the OECD Recommendation on Public Integrity, such an open culture of organisational integrity:

- invests in integrity leadership to demonstrate a public sector organisation's commitment to integrity
- promotes a merit-based, professional, public sector dedicated to public-service values and good governance
- provides sufficient information, training, guidance and timely advice for public officials to apply public integrity standards in the workplace
- supports an open organisational culture within the public sector responsive to integrity concerns and where ethical dilemmas, public integrity concerns, and errors can be discussed freely
- applies an internal control and risk management framework to safeguard integrity.

As mentioned in Chapter 1, the existence of a dedicated unit for public entity does not entail that this unit should be responsible for implementing all activities related to integrity itself. Quite on the contrary, it is important to understand and strengthen the role of "complementary" internal integrity actors with key support functions such as human resource management, transparency and citizen engagement or investigation and sanctioning of integrity violations. Indeed, ensuring a merit-based recruitment, general capacity building as well as incorporating integrity measures throughout the HR management cycle is a core responsibility of the HR units, for example. Similarly, ensuring appropriate responses to all suspected violations of public integrity standards by public officials and all others involved in the violations should not be carried out by the UGI, but by the Federal Inspectors. Nonetheless, in both cases, the UGI plays a role in ensuring coherence with other elements of the Integrity Programme.

As such, the revised guidance to the UGI could focus, again, on three core competences, which will be developed in more detail below:

- Co-ordination, planning and monitoring of the Integrity Programmes.
- Providing guidance and training on areas on public integrity, including for example guidance and trainings on values, dealing with ethical dilemmas, developing skills for ethical leadership.
- Provide guidance and support integrity risk management, including management of conflict of interests.

Co-ordinating, planning and monitoring

As indicated by Figure 2.1 above, the UGI have spent most their time and resources on co-ordinating and establishing the Integrity Programme. Indeed, a core function of the UGI is to co-ordinate efforts regarding the design of the integrity plans, lead internal co-ordination between the different integrity units and monitor the implementation of these plans to provide a degree of assurance for the head of the entities regarding compliance with the standards and policies. This includes, for example, alerting the head of the entity to the need of strengthening any of the areas relevant for ensuring an open culture of integrity.

Internal co-ordination is a challenging and time-consuming task. Figure 2.2 shows some of the main challenges to an effective internal co-ordination. According to the responses received, confirmed in a Focus Group carried out with selected UGI, a main challenge relates to the fact that today most UGI are not dedicated units, but have to carry out other functions, not related to public integrity and this aspect will be discussed in the section below (see also Figure 2.3). A further challenge relates to the administrative burden that comes along with co-ordination, such as the need to seek for approval from hierarchies before agreeing to goals committing two or more units or before making commitments of time and resources. Finally, the answers show that the quality of co-ordination depends heavily on the individuals that happen to be in place in the other units. As a popular saying states: "Everybody agrees that co-ordination is necessary, but nobody likes being co-ordinated". Indeed, this last point indicates the relevance of ensuring that the UGI has sufficient convening power to ensure an effective co-ordination, which should be reflected in its position in the organigram. Again, this aspect will be picked up below.

Figure 2.2. Perceived challenges to an effective internal co-ordination on public integrity amongst selected UGI

(1 = not a challenge, 2 = somewhat of a challenge, 3 = a moderate challenge, 4 = severe challenge)

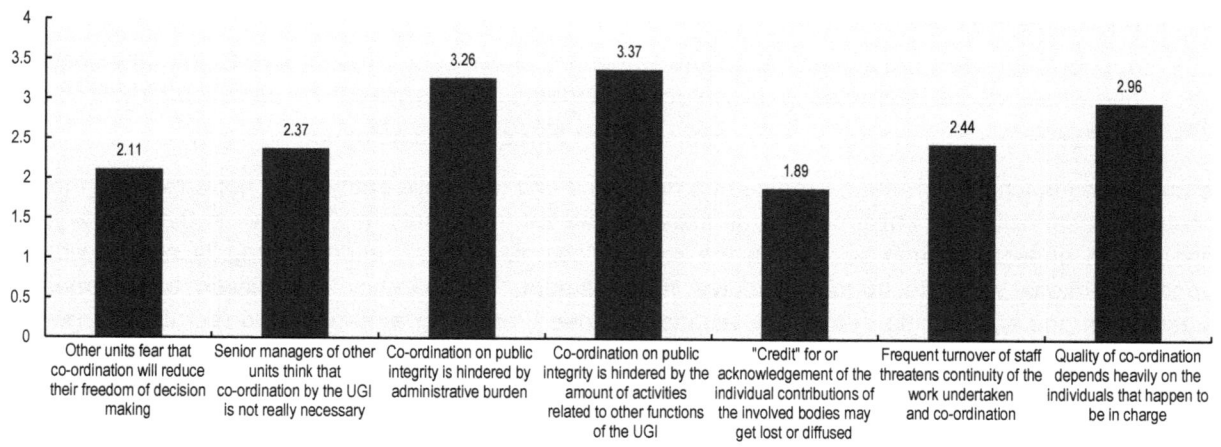

Note: The OECD questionnaire was sent to 35 UGI, from which 30 responses were received. For this Figure, 27 answers could be used. The sample is thus not representative but indicative and has been supported by qualitative interviews and a focus group.
Source: OECD Survey 2020.

Co-ordination is of particular relevance for another core function of the UGI, which is leading the development of an institutional Integrity Plan. The cross-cutting relevance of integrity for safeguarding the achievement of the mission of the public entity and its policy goals call for an effective implementation of integrity measures throughout the public entity. To ensure relevance and ownership, the UGI should not focus so much on the content of the Integrity Plans and what exactly other units should do, but rather promote a bottom-up approach through a participative internal planning methodology to develop the Integrity Plans.

As mentioned above, 100% of the UGI have already approved the Integrity Plans, but it remains unclear to what extend these Plans were elaborated in such a participative way. In fact, while the Guide provided to the UGI does highlight that the Integrity Plan should respond to identified integrity risks and be approved by the highest authority of the federal entity, it does however neither provide guidance on a participative planning process nor emphasise this aspect (CGU, 2018[1]). While the CGU could consider elaborating guidance on how to conduct such a planning process and help building the required competences (see the section on the CGU), the UGI should already aim at using the development of the Integrity Plans as a core co-ordination instrument to raise awareness, build ownership and promote the implementation of targeted measures.

For example, the French Anticorruption Guide emphasises the relevance of a participative planning process to ensure the accuracy of assessing the specific organisational integrity risks (Agence Française

Anticorruption, 2020[4]). The Guide underlines that, when conducting corruption risk mapping, entities should hold discussions, in form of collective workshops and/or individual interviews, with staff members from all hierarchical levels and all relevant functions chosen for their operational command of these processes. These discussions allow participants to freely express their views and are written up in reports. They aim to identify, per process, the risk scenarios to which the public sector entity is exposed in terms of its activities and certain lines of work in order to design tailored measures to manage these risks more effectively.

Indeed, in Brazil, the CGU Guide emphasises that Integrity Plans should be based on an integrity risk analysis, which is an opportunity to ensure a clear theory of change underlying the measures included in the Integrity Plans. This allows to identify measures addressing and mitigating the identified risks and contributing to achieving the overall objective, which is achieving behavioural and cultural change within the entity. A related task consists in the establishment of relevant and actionable indicators. This process, again, allows to clarify what exactly is the desired change that the public entity wants to achieve, can avoid proposing activities just for the sake of "doing something" and facilitates the monitoring and the evaluation process of the Integrity Plans. At an early stage, "change" is likely to be defined mostly on process and product levels (unit is in place, channels have been established, trainings have been implemented etc.). In the medium to long term, more ambitious, outcome indicators, based on regular surveys or administrative data, could be identified and added.

In addition, experience shows that goals that are not included explicitly into the organisational planning, budgets and internal accountability mechanisms, such as performance evaluations, are unlikely to be taken seriously by managers. While it makes sense to have an Integrity Plan separate from the "normal" strategic and operational planning of the public entity to ensure visibility and raise awareness, the Integrity Plans should be aligned with the institutional planning and include clear responsibilities, objectives and resources to ensure their implementation.

Finally, co-ordination is also a key element of the monitoring function of the UGI. Indeed, it is important not to confuse monitoring with ensuring compliance. The core objective of monitoring is to identify challenges and opportunities in a timely manner to inform decisions and enable adjustments during implementation (OECD, 2017[5]). As such, monitoring should always be understood as contributing to an effective public management and not be perceived as a control mechanism aimed at naming and shaming. Monitoring thus needs to be clearly communicated as a joint exercise to analyse and overcome challenges and linked with the process of decision-making and implementation. To achieve this, clear mechanisms and procedures to discuss progress should be established internally by the UGI, for instance through regular meetings to discuss progress and challenges. Such a task requires specialised staff with knowledge about planning and monitoring, but also a sound level of diplomatic and communication skills. This is, again, an argument in favour of having a dedicated UGI where such skills can be cultivated and where this task is not at risk of being confounded with other non-integrity related responsibilities of the unit that took over the responsibilities of acting as UGI. In addition, the CGU could consider providing guidance in relation to the process of monitoring and help building the required competences, similar to those required for leading the planning process (see the section on the CGU below).

Providing guidance and training to public servants on public integrity

Both the OECD Recommendation on Public Integrity and the OECD Recommendation on Public Service Leadership and Capability are emphasising the relevance of a values-driven culture and leadership in the civil service. Values are providing the moral compass for doing the right thing. They are the foundation for achieving organisational cultures of integrity throughout the public sector and are enabling a working environment that is more innovative, productive and, ultimately, also more ethical and humane. Providing guidance on shared values and their relevance for public servants is therefore a core aspect of promoting public integrity (OECD, 2020[3]).

A second core responsibility of the UGI thus relates to promoting guidance and training on matters relating to the Integrity Programme, as indicated in the SIPEF. In particular, this means providing ad hoc guidance as well as trainings aimed at promoting an understanding of the practical relevance of values for the day-to-day work and for managing conflict of interest and enabling the capacities of public servants to deal with ethical dilemmas.

Currently, the Code of Professional Ethics (Decree 1171/1994) has been the main instrument setting standards of conduct for public officials in Brazil. In addition, several federal entities have implemented their own code of ethics and/or conduct to complement the Code of Professional Ethics. However, the Code of Professional Ethics is drafted as a legal document and does not lend itself to be useful as a moral compass in day-to-day work. Indeed, behavioural research suggests that a set of values or key principles ideally should have no more than seven elements to be easily memorised (OECD, 2018[6]; Miller, 1955[7]). Rather than adding another legal layer, values should above all be of practical relevance and memorable for public employees and target the informal level and social aspects that are shaping human behaviour. Driven by this consideration, countries such as Australia and Colombia have reviewed their approach to ethics codes and significantly reduced the number of values (Box 2.1). Similarly, the UK Civil Service Code outlines just four civil service values, Law 2016 outlines four core values for the public duties in France, and the Danish "Kodex VII" defines seven central duties to guide civil servants.

> ### Box 2.1. Revising Ethics Codes: The experiences of Australia and Colombia
>
> **Revision of the Australian Public Service (APS) values**
>
> In the past, the Australian Public Service Commission used a statement of values expressed as a list of 15 rules. In 2010, the Advisory Group on Reform of Australian Government Administration released its report "Ahead of the Game", which recognised the relevance of a robust values framework and a values-based leadership in driving performance. The report recommended that the APS values could be revised, tightened, and made more memorable. The values were updated to follow the acronym "I CARE": Impartial; Committed to service; Accountable; Respectful; Ethical.
>
> **The Colombian Integrity Code**
>
> In 2016, the Colombian Administrative Department of Public Administration initiated a process to define a General Integrity Code. Through a participatory exercise involving more than 25 000 public servants through different mechanisms, five core values were selected: Honesty; Respect; Commitment; Diligence; Justice. In addition, each public entity has the possibility to integrate up to two additional values or principles to respond to organisational, regional and/or sectorial specificities.
>
> Source: Australian Public Service Commission, https://www.apsc.gov.au/working-aps/aps-employees-and-managers/aps-values; Departamento Administrativo de la Función Pública, Colombia https://www.funcionpublica.gov.co/web/eva/codigo-integridad.

Inspired by such international good practices and with support from the OECD in the context of this project, the CGU has led in 2020 a participative process to identify the core values of the Federal Public Service in Brazil (*Valores do Serviço Público Federal*). After an extensive consultation process, civil servants identified which are today the seven Values of the Federal public service (Box 2.2).

> **Box 2.2. The 7 Values of the Federal Public Service in Brazil**
>
> The Comptroller General of the Union (CGU), in partnership with the Organization for Economic Co-operation and Development (OECD), led the process of identifying the core Values of the Federal Public Service. The initiative was carried out by an online voting procedure, through which federal public servants throughout Brazil could choose and propose which values they consider should guide the culture of the federal public administration.
>
> During October 2020, the CGU launched the online survey inviting all interested federal civil servants to participate. The Integrity Management Units (UGI) were instrumental in promoting the survey and mobilising the participation. In this first survey, 33 407 public servants participated and proposed overall 93 809 values. Then, the CGU, together with the OECD cleaned and grouped the values indicated by the public servants to reduce the number. The top ten values were selected and validated in a process including the participation of representatives from the private sector and civil society. A second survey, with 25 637 participating public servants, then reduced the 10 values to the 7 final values, which are: Integrity, Professionalism, Impartiality, Justice, Engagement, Kindness and Public Vocation. Each value comes along with a brief description of what it means, which provided the opportunity to add similar values that pointed into the same direction.
>
> The idea behind the participative process is to ensure that the values represent what public servants themselves feel should guide their personal development, work routines, skills and organisational climate. After the launch of the values in April 2021, the CGU and the UGI have been start working on promoting the values and it is planned to develop a toolbox and material to support the promotion and application of the values.
>
> Source: OECD and CGU, more information available at https://www.gov.br/cgu/pt-br/valores-do-servico-publico

These Values, through their clarity and practical relevance, provide an excellent entry point to promote a values-based approach to public integrity in Brazil. The ongoing revision of the Code of Professional Ethics and the Code of Conduct of the High Federal Administration mentioned in Chapter 1, provides an excellent opportunity to make these values the foundation for unified guidance to public servants from all levels with respect to public integrity.

Furthermore, the values can be used by the CGU and the UGI for trainings and to provide guidance on reflecting about ethical dilemmas, managing conflict of interest, including dealing with nepotism or how public servants should relate with lobbyists, for example. In particular, the CGU and the UGI could aim at promoting integrity leadership in the public entities by raising awareness and developing skills for leaders at all levels of public managements (OECD, forthcoming[8]).

Public servants, in particular, need guidance and support on how to deal with ethical dilemmas. Ethical dilemmas are a key challenge for integrity policies, as dilemmas arise in cases where there are no clear legal "right" of "wrong" answers or where there may be conflicts between different values or principles. For instance, the ability to regulate, apply coercive power, and control systems and processes that have a broad impact on society (e.g. defence, health, social welfare) increasingly blurs the boundaries between public sector organisations and their complex partnerships with other sectors, which can lead to ethical dilemmas (OECD, 2020[3]). In Australia, for example, the REFLECT model provides public officials with general sequenced steps and reflections on how to proceed when confronted with ethical dilemmas (Box 2.3). Brazil could aim at developing similar guidance, using the new values as a moral compass.

> **Box 2.3. Guiding public officials in facing ethical dilemmas in Australia**
>
> The Australian Government developed and implemented strategies to enhance ethics and accountability in the Australian Public Service (APS). To help public servants in their decision making process when facing ethical dilemmas, the Australian Public Service Commission developed a decision making model.
>
> The model follows the acronym REFLECT and follows six steps:
>
> - REcognise a potential issue or problem
> - Find relevant information
> - Linger at the 'fork in the road' (talking it through)
> - Evaluate the options
> - Come to a decision
> - Take time to reflect
>
> Source: Office of the Merit Protection Commissioner (2009), "Ethical Decision Making", https://legacy.apsc.gov.au/ethical-decision-making

Supporting and guiding Integrity risk management, including managing conflict of interest

Implementing risk management in the public sector is a challenge; implementing integrity risk management perhaps even more (OECD, 2019[9]). In fact, many countries struggle with implementing the conceptual frameworks and promoting a culture of integrity risk management in public entities. In Brazil's Federal Executive, integrity risk management became mandatory for all federal public entities with Decree 9203/2017. Integrity risk management is a key element of the Integrity Programmes and the Integrity Plans and now of the SIPEF. Integrity risks are the foundation on which to elaborate the Integrity Plans. Along these lines, a third core responsibility of the UGI, as a unit of the second line of defence, is supporting public managers in integrity risk identification and management.

By the time of this report, according to the monitoring platform of the CGU, 89% of all federal entities have realised a first integrity risk assessment. The CGU provides a methodology for integrity risk assessments, laid out in the Practical Guide to Integrity Risk Management (CGU, 2018[10]). The document provides guidance on the implementation of integrity risk management, raises awareness and delivers concrete "how-to" steps as well as insights on generic integrity risks and cases. The Guide reinforces the notion that managing integrity risks is the responsibility of the managers. Specifically, it requires that managers establish, monitor and improve risk management and internal control systems. This includes the identification, evaluation, treatment, monitoring, and critical analysis of risks that may affect the achievement of organisational objectives when fulfilling the institutional mission. However, CGU's ongoing evaluation of the UGI and the OECD fact-finding revealed that integrity risk management in federal entities not always follows the CGU methodology and that there are significant differences in levels of maturity and in promoting risk management cultures amongst public managers. The methodology for integrity risk management proposed by the CGU, as well as the challenge of promoting a culture of integrity risk management are considered in depth in another OECD report in the context of this project (OECD, forthcoming[11]).

In general, the UGI can play a key role in promoting an integrity risk management culture, both through their mandate to provide guidance and trainings and through the specific mandate to coordinate the management of risks to integrity (see Box 1.4 in Chapter 1). Indeed, the focus groups with UGI, the interviews and the responses to the OECD Survey evidenced that integrity risk management still faces challenges in the day-to-day implementation. While it is true that there is a degree of heterogeneity of the maturity of integrity risk management in the Federal executive, with some public entities being more advanced than others, there is an overarching acknowledgement that there is still a long way to go to normalise integrity risk management.

As such, the UGI could promote a better understanding of the relevance of integrity risk management and support to managers in carrying out integrity risk assessments. This responsibility is key as the quality of the Integrity Plans and the proposed internal controls depend heavily on the quality of the integrity risk assessments in the first place. On the one hand, the UGI should be able to clearly communicate about the rationale of integrity risks and contribute to demystify the concept and to reduce fears and misunderstandings related to them. On the other hand, the UGI need to develop skills in making integrity risk assessments as simple as possible to managers.

A particular risk where misunderstandings amongst public servants is particularly high is the area of conflicts of interest. Of course, effectively managing conflict of interest corresponds to managing one of the major integrity risks, and it includes sensitive areas such as how to deal with contracting friends or family, communicating with outside stakeholders that have vested interests in the decisions, actions or non-actions of the public entity or outside activities. The 2003 OECD Guidelines for Managing Conflict of Interest aim at helping countries to promote a public service culture where conflicts of interest are properly identified and resolved or managed, in an appropriately transparent and timely way, without unduly inhibiting the effectiveness and efficiency of the public organisations concerned (OECD, 2004[12]). The G20 High-Level Principles for Preventing and Managing 'Conflict of Interest' in the Public Sector encourage countries to nurture an open organisational culture in the public sector, taking steps to promote the pro-active identification and avoidance of potential conflict-of-interest situations by public officials (World Bank, 2018[13]).

Essentially, the effectiveness of policies for managing conflict of interest rests upon the understanding that public servants have about the concept of conflicting interests and their capacity to identify when being in such a situation and understanding the risks related to this situation. As such, similar to the challenge of promoting a risk management culture amongst public managers, managing conflict of interest requires much more than normative frameworks and tools to submit potential conflict of interest situation. Again, the UGI can and should play a key role in promoting this cultural change that requires more than putting in place channels for consultations or requiring public servants to fill out interest declarations.

To ensure the impact of the UGI, Brazil should consider harmonising their design to align their organisational structure and capacities with their responsibilities

As mentioned in Chapter 1, the current framework allows that other units can perform the functions of the UGI. This means that the position of the UGI in the internal governance structure can vary and that, typically, the UGI is a unit where integrity has just been added to other existing responsibilities. Figure 2.3 shows the distribution of units carrying out the functions of the UGI. Strikingly, 78 out of the 186 entities at federal level have not reported back on their location in the public entity. For several reasons, this currently undermines significantly the potential impact of the UGI and the role they could play in carrying out the functions attributed to them within the SIPEF.

Figure 2.3. Units designated as Integrity Managament Units in the Brazilian federal executive

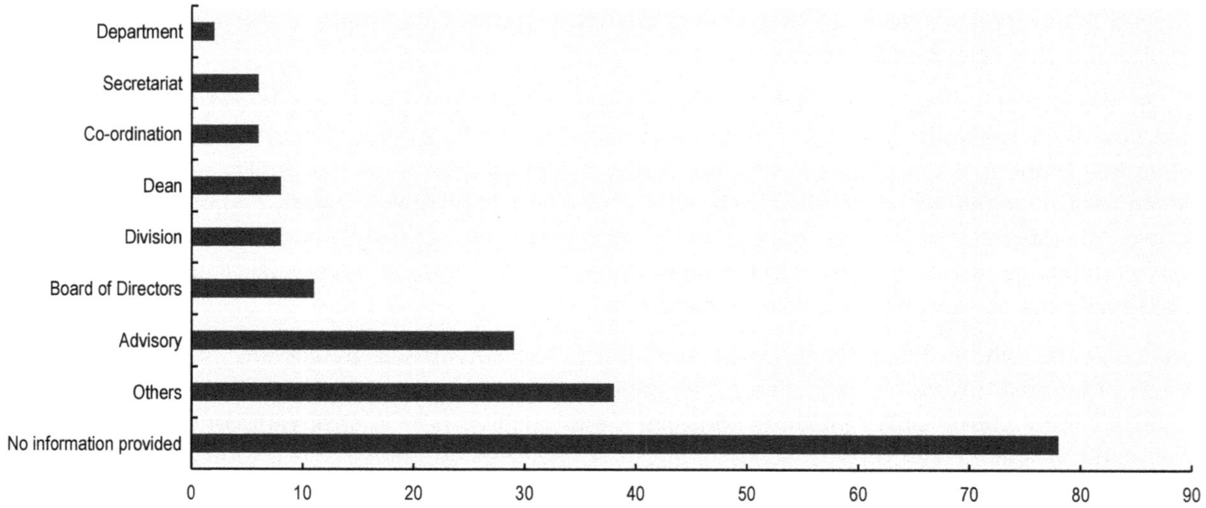

Category	Count
Department	2
Secretariat	6
Co-ordination	6
Dean	8
Division	8
Board of Directors	11
Advisory	29
Others	38
No information provided	78

Source: CGU, data extracted from http://paineis.cgu.gov.br/integridadepublica

First, as mentioned in Chapter 1, the UGI should be separated from any functions related to auditing or enforcement to clarify institutional responsibilities and to allow a clear focus on prevention and the promotion of open cultures of integrity (OECD, 2018[6]). Currently, the CGU recommends that the functions of the UGI should not be carried out by the internal audit units or internal control areas, for example. However, along the same lines, any other unit related to integrity policies, such as the federal inspectorates (*corregedorias*), the ombudsmen (*ouvidorias*) or the Ethics Commissions should be maintained separate from the UGI. This also avoids potential conflicts between the requisites for sectorial units of the respective federal systems.

Second, the OECD fact-finding indicates that the UGI themselves perceive the fact of not being a dedicated unit with professionalised staff as a weakness. During the focus group, they mentioned the need to have professionalised staff that is exclusively dedicated to integrity. They emphasised that they are often lacking the specific capacities needed to carry out their work and that they are often overwhelmed by tasks that are unrelated to integrity but also part of their responsibilities. They further perceive that not being a dedicated unit reflects a lack of commitment by senior management and reported that the situation makes difficult to access to the higher administration. Overall, they perceive that the support from the highest authority correlates with the position of the UGI in the organisational structure. Not having a direct access affects the ability of the UGI to communicate with the highest authority, playing their role as advisor, but also undermines the convening power of the UGI to articulate the Integrity Programme with other units, as mentioned previously.

Indeed, the commitment of both the entity's head and the senior leadership, identified as a key component of the Integrity Programmes and the SIPEF, in order to gain credibility, needs to be reflected in the continuity of integrity policies and in dedicating sufficient human and financial resources to effectively implement the SIPEF beyond a check-the-box approach (Brinkerhoff, 2000[14]). In particular, the allocation of resources should be proportionate to the public sector entity's integrity risk profile. Finally, from a behavioural insights perspective, again, the fact that the UGI is sharing responsibilities for integrity with other non-integrity related functions, reduces the salience of integrity in the organisation and makes it more difficult for public servants to clearly identify and associate the UGI as such (OECD, 2018[6]).

Therefore, the CGU could consider taking the recent SIPEF as an opportunity to rethink the organisational underpinning of the system within federal entities and require the establishment of dedicated UGI. If, as recommended above, the UGI take over the preventive functions of the Ethics Commissions and the Federal Inspectorates are responsible for investigating and sanctioning integrity violations, the UGI could take the place of the Ethics Commissions in the organigram (see Chapter 1). Seen from another perspective, and similar to what has been recommended to Mexico, the Ethics Commissions could be transformed into UGI, but as units with permanent staff, where the competences and skills required for the UGI can be developed over time (OECD, 2019[15]; OECD, 2017[16]).

The dedicated unit should report directly to the highest authority and to the CGU, which exercises a technical supervision of the activities related to the Integrity Programmes and the UGI as emphasised in the SIPEF (see next section) to guarantee that it can carry out its functions of alerting to the need of strengthening any of the integrity areas. In addition, a certain degree of administrative autonomy, for example when recruiting personnel, and financial autonomy through a specific budget, would allow a more effective work of the UGI. Furthermore, as in France, to enhance the effectiveness of the UGI's work, it would be useful to guarantee its access to all relevant information regarding the public sector entity's activities (and consequently, their associated risks) and its capacity to have a real influence on the other departments (Agence Française Anticorruption, 2020[4]). This autonomy, along with the second accountability channel towards the CGU, will help to guarantee a certain degree of independence and power to address also more sensitive risks and challenges with management.

To sum up, as dedicated units, the UGI would be able to address several challenges and current weaknesses identified above and significantly enhance their capacities to deliver their mandate and functions.

In particular, as highlighted in Box 1.6 in Chapter 1, this would allow the following advantages:

- Promote internal clarity and visibility within the federal entity with respect to who is responsible for supporting the promotion of public integrity. Currently, there is a risk that public servants unconsciously associate the UGI with the other non-integrity related functions of the area that took the responsibilities of the UGI. This could make more difficult to communicate clearly on public integrity. In fact, the fact-finding evidenced that public officials and other areas within public entities currently not always understand the mandate and functions of the UGI. A dedicated UGI, in turn, would be able to develop a clear profile and own identity.

- Facilitate the function of advising the highest authority, articulating the Integrity Programme and steering the development and monitoring of the Integrity Plans. As already mentioned, co-ordination requires a certain degree of convening power to ask for participation of or information from other internal units. This is more likely if the UGI is a dedicated unit that reports directly to the head of the entity. For example, in Paraguay, the Law mandates that heads of the Anti-Corruption Units report directly to the head of the respective institution.

- Building the different sets of competences and skills required to promote open culture of public integrity (co-ordination, planning, monitoring, guidance and integrity risk management). To develop the required skills over time and allow a learning process, the UGI should ideally count with permanent staff, recruited as career civil servants with a stable position. This would also allow the development of a relationship build on trust between UGI staff and staff from other units within the entity. This is indispensable for an effective co-ordination and for public servants to feel comfortable to approach the UGI about any doubts or concerns.

The advantages of structuring the SIPEF and harmonising the design of the UGI shall not disregard the fact that there are diverse realities in the federal executive; diversity with respect to the size of entities and their resources, but also diversity in integrity risks that they face. The establishment of the UGI should take existing resources and proportionality into account to limit additional bureaucratic layers. Similar to what has been recommended in Mexico or Peru, Brazil could thus consider allowing small entities to have smaller UGI; for very small entities, e.g. with staff under 100, it could even be considered to exceptionally allow an Integrity Manager as a unit instead of a team (OECD, 2019[17]; OECD, 2019[15]). Nonetheless, the decision about the size of the UGI ideally should not to be taken by the public entity alone. Rather the CGU could support and validate the proposals from federal entities and, in case of disagreement, could be able to veto a proposal and impose the design that it deems pertinent.

Finally, although not covered by the obligation of Decree 9203/2017 and 10756/2021, some administrative units, due to their size, complexity and related integrity risks, could benefit from establishing an Integrity Programme and an UGI. This is the case for federal hospitals and other administrative units attached to a Ministry, such as Federal Police, the Federal Highway Police and the Internal Revenue Service. Under the SIPEF, the CGU therefore could continue making efforts to foster the implementation of Integrity Programmes in such administrative units. In addition, the CGU could consider including generic guidance concerning such units into the SIPEF, by revising the Decree 10756/2021, and request the implementation of Integrity Programmes in such administrative units, following certain characteristics such as size and integrity risks.

Enhancing CGU's role as the Central Body of the Public Integrity System in the Federal Executive

The CGU could consider revisiting the responsibilities of the Directorate for Integrity Promotion and the Directorate for the Prevention of Corruption to clarify their role within the SIPEF

The Secretariat of Transparency and Corruption Prevention (*Secretaria de Transparência e Prevenção da Corrupção*, STPC) in the CGU has been playing a key role in promoting public and private integrity and fostering transparency and social control in the federal public administration. Furthermore, it proposes and develops measures to identify and prevent conflict of interest situations and serves as executive secretary of the Council for Public Transparency and Combating Corruption (*Conselho de Transparência Pública e Combate à Corrupção*, CTPCC).

Recently, the STPC has been designated as the Central Body of the SIPEF with the responsibilities for establishing the rules and procedures for the exercise of the competences of the units that are part of SIPEF and the attributions of the directors for the management of Integrity Programmes. The STPC shall guide activities related to risk management for integrity and carry out communication and training actions related to integrity as well as coordinate activities that require joint actions by the UGI. As oversight body of the SIPEF, the STPC exercises the technical supervision of activities related to the Integrity Programmes managed by the UGI, monitors and evaluates the performance of the UGI and shall inform the federal entities of facts or situations that may compromise their Integrity Programmes and may recommend the adoption of the necessary remedial measures.

The STPC is currently divided into three Directorates:

- The Directorate for Transparency and Social Control (*Diretoria de Transparência e Controle Social*, DTCS) is responsible for policies related to open government, transparency, citizen education and social control (for an in-depth discussion of the DTCS, see OECD Open Government Review (OECD, forthcoming[18])).
- The Directorate for Integrity Promotion (*Diretoria de Promoção da Integridade*, DPI), which has a unit dedicated to public integrity and a unit dedicated to the promotion of Integrity within the private sector.

- The Directorate for the Prevention of Corruption (*Diretoria de Prevenção da Corrupção*, DPC), which has a unit dedicated to public ethics and prevention of conflict of interest and a unit responsible for innovation and corruption prevention.

Table 2.1 provides an overview of the current responsibilities of the DPI and the DPC, which are the most relevant Directorates from the perspective of public integrity and the issues discussed so far.

Table 2.1. Responsibilities of CGU Departments for Integrity Promotion and Prevention of Corruption

Department for Integrity Promotion	The Department for the Prevention of Corruption
<ul><li>developing, supporting and fostering initiatives to increase integrity in the public and private sectors;</li><li>prioritising integrity promotion initiatives;</li><li>promoting, supporting and disseminating studies and research on methodologies and tools to strengthen integrity systems, programmes and plans in the federal executive branch and private legal entities</li><li>establish guidelines, recommendations and methodologies related to the implementation, application, evaluation and supervision of integrity programmes.</li><li>establish guidelines for monitoring integrity programmes</li><li>supporting in matters related to private integrity, including compliance and corporate governance;</li><li>monitor the implementation of the integrity programmes of public entities</li><li>establish guidelines for the evaluation of integrity programmes and plans of federal entities.</li></ul>	<ul><li>proposing the standardisation and systematisation of procedures and normative acts related to activities related to the prevention of corruption, public ethics and conflicts of interest;</li><li>proposing and developing measures to identify and prevent conflicts of interest situations</li><li>promoting activities and studies on ethical conduct within the federal executive branch;</li><li>formulating, promoting, implementing and evaluating the principles, guidelines, programmes, services and priority issues related to the prevention of corruption</li><li>fostering, guiding and stimulating the development and improvement of solutions, services and processes for the prevention of corruption;</li></ul>

Source: Portaria 3553/2019.

The fact-finding of this project indicates that re-thinking the division of labour within the STPC, in particular between the current DPI and the DPC, could significantly enhance its impact by ensuring coherence and avoiding frictions and overlaps. Indeed, similar to the recommendations above related to the Federal Ethics Management System and the Public Integrity System, the distinction between public integrity, public ethics, preventing conflict-of-interest and corruption is conceptually blurred and leads to a lack of clarity about responsibilities and risks of mixed messages, misunderstandings and therefore potentially a waste of scarce resources.

On the one hand, the CGU should consider strengthening the DPI by streamlining the tasks related to public integrity and the SIPEF under its responsibility. Indeed, the DPI has established itself as the unit leading public integrity and co-ordinating as well as supporting the UGI. In line and coherent with the recommendations in Chapter 1 and with respect to the UGI, a separation between public integrity, public ethics, managing conflict of interest and integrity risk management does not make sense and is not helpful to provide clarity for public servants about the concepts and the responsibilities for guidance. As such, it is recommended that these aspects are bundled under the umbrella of public integrity and that the DPI leads the development of related policies and guidance.

On the other hand, the DPC has recently made progress in promoting surveys and exploring the use of innovative tools related to the use of data and data analytics or joint research projects with academia. The CGU could therefore consider strengthening the current DPC by building on this and expanding its capacities as a unit responsible for providing methodological and research advice to the DPI and the DTCS. This could include, for example, commissioning and supervising research projects, support for designing and implementing surveys, identifying and analysing relevant data, developing new analytical tools and providing methodological support for conducting experiments and impact evaluations. All these areas require specific skills that could significantly support the work of the operational DPI and DTCS. In addition, the CGU could consider changing the name of the DPC to reflect this new focus.

Finally, while the adoption and enforcement of state and municipal anti-corruption and integrity standards is a competence of local entities, CGU's DTC started to provide support and guidance to states and municipalities in the implementation of federal laws on anti-corruption and integrity, internal control, transparency, and access to information (Box 2.4). Indeed, when federal laws refer to the national interest, they shall inform regulation in all 26 states, the Federal District and the 5,570 Brazilian municipalities. That is the case, for example, of the Anti-Corruption Law (Law No. 12,846, of August 1st, 2013), which provides for the objective administrative and civil liability of legal entities for violations of standards against the public administration and which should be implemented by the Federal Government, States and Municipalities in their constitutional jurisdictions. As of December 2020, 21 States had already regulated the Anti-corruption Law, either partly or in full. Therefore, the CGU could continue building on these efforts to promote a mainstreaming beyond the federal executive branch and reach states and municipalities.

Box 2.4. CGU support in the implementation of integrity and anti-corruption standards in states and municipalities

In 2017, the CGU released two booklets to support states and municipalities to regulate Law 12846/2013 (CGU, 2017[19]; CGU, 2017[20]). This material is part of the series "Transparent Municipality", which makes available, in digital form, publications aimed at improving the management of federal resources in municipalities. Additional support provided to states and municipalities include videos as well as in person and virtual capacity building events on conflict of interests, nepotism, integrity risk managements.

In 2019, the CGU also launched the Brazil TEAM Program to assist states and municipalities in improving public management and strengthening the fight against corruption around three axes (Transparency, Integrity and Social Participation), in particular:

- To substantially reduce corruption and bribery in all its forms.
- Develop effective, accountable and transparent institutions at all levels.
- Ensure responsive, inclusive, participatory and representative decision-making at all levels.

Source: (CGU, 2017[20]); (CGU, 2017[19]); and https://www.gov.br/cgu/pt-br/assuntos/transparencia-publica/time-brasil/trilhas

---

By providing guidance and support, CGU's STPC is key to enhance and ensure the impact of the new Public Integrity System of the Federal Executive (SIPEF)

As the central organ of the SIPEF, the relationship between the STPC and the sectorial units, the UGI, is key to make the SIPEF work. The STPC provides directions and guidance to the UGI, but it is important to emphasise that the UGI also can provide key information from the bottom-up to the CGU. Indeed, the UGI are closer to the realities in their respective federal entities and therefore to the specific challenges and opportunities. To work as a system, the STPC should ensure to acknowledge this two-way relationship by providing opportunities for feedback from the UGI when designing new regulations or policies and by allowing a degree of flexibility to the UGI in adapting the directives and guidance issued by the CGU to their realities and priorities.

In line with the recommendations aimed at strengthening the UGI above, the STPC could therefore continue and build on its current efforts to strengthen the UGI and focus in particular on the following five core work streams.

- **Provide guidelines, trainings and ad hoc support on integrity policies.** In line with the suggested focus of the UGI on promoting open cultures of organisational integrity mentioned above, this support by the DPI could focus on:
    - providing guidance and building capacities on how to steer and co-ordinate an internal, participative planning exercise
    - building a theory of change to avoid a check-the-box approach focusing on implementing and complying with a series of actions without having a clear vision of the desired change
    - skills and tools to facilitate the monitoring of the implementation of the Integrity Plans
    - the elements of an open organisational culture of integrity, to provide conceptual clarity and coherence across the federal executive branch and to suggest ways to promote and support the implementation of the different elements
    - how to provide ad hoc advice and guidance to public servants that seek support or clarifications on integrity issues (e.g. guidance on identifying and managing conflict of interest, ethical dilemmas etc.)
    - how to promote integrity risk management cultures and how to use the information of the integrity risk assessments to inform their decisions and activities.
- **Support integrity risk management of the UGI.** The STPC, by collecting the risk assessments from the federal entities and relying on the feedback from the UGI can carry out analysis that go beyond single entities (e.g. sectors, regions, or standard high-risk processes such as public procurement or human resource management). The STPC could complement these risk assessments by using data from other sources, carrying out advanced data analytics and feed this information back to the UGI to support and fine-tune their own risk analysis (OECD, forthcoming[11]). Within the STPC, ideally, the DPI identifies the needs and seeks support for the analysis of the data by the DPC, or the new name of this Directorate.
- **Strengthen the evidence base to support the UGI and the SIPEF.** The STPC could identify relevant data from administrative sources and surveys and identify gaps where additional data could be collected. In particular, the STPC could consider developing a standard survey to measure the integrity climate in the public entity, including aspect related to integrity leadership, to support and inform the UGI (OECD, forthcoming[8]). Again, the content part should be led by DPI with methodological support for survey design and data analysis from the DPC.
- **Continue to support and promote exchanges between UGI, leveraging new technologies.** The COVID-19 crisis triggered and showed both the opportunities and limitations of the use of online discussion platforms, videoconferences and webinars. The STPC could consider to learn from this experiment and prepare for a future where the in-person and online meetings will co-exist and can be leveraged. In particular, the STPC could consider continue its current practice to promote capacity building and dialogue through webinars. In addition, regular online network meetings between the UGI could significantly facilitate the exchange on common challenges and good practices and be an opportunity for the STPC to hear back from the UGI.
- **Monitor the implementation of the Integrity Programmes and regularly evaluate the SIPEF.** Similar to the role of the UGI in monitoring the Integrity Plans at institutional level, the STPC should continue monitoring and evaluating the Integrity Programmes, the UGI and now, more generally, the SIPEF. Though interconnected, it is important to distinguish between monitoring and evaluation.
    - **Monitoring** corresponds to a routinized process of evidence gathering and reporting to ensure that resources are adequately spent, outputs are successfully delivered, and milestones and targets are met (OECD, 2020[21]). Again, it is important here that the STPC does not confuse monitoring with control (OECD, 2017[5]) and aims at promoting a constructive dialogue with the UGI about challenges and solutions. Currently, the public monitoring platform provided by the

CGU (paineis.cgu.gov.br/integridadepublica) focuses on establishing units and procedures, reflecting the early stages of the Integrity Programmes. The STPC could thus consider adding indicators that also capture the quality of or the use of these unites and procedures. Furthermore, the STPC could consider establishing an *internal* monitoring mechanism to allow for honest reporting by the UGI, while maintaining accountability towards the whole of society through a public platform with more generic indicators.

o **Evaluation**, in turn, is an assessment of an ongoing or completed initiative, its design, implementation and results. Evaluations determine the relevance and fulfilment of objectives, efficiency, effectiveness, impact and sustainability, as well as the worth or significance of a policy (OECD, 2020[21]). As such, the STPC should continue its good practice reflected in the current, ongoing, evaluation of the UGI through surveys and in-depth interviews, allowing for a learning exercise and an incremental strengthening of the SIPEF over time.

Finally, given that the CGU is also part of the SIPEF, as its central organ, it may be interesting to consider a regular external independent evaluation of the overall system to identify and address possible shortcomings of the SIPEF. A recent OECD study demonstrated that generally, countries show strong commitment to policy evaluation. Some countries have embedded policy evaluations in their constitutions, and around two-thirds of responding countries have developed some kind of legal framework for policy evaluation. Similarly, most countries have adopted guidelines on policy evaluation applicable across government (OECD, 2020[21]).

References

Agence Française Anticorruption (2020), *The French Anti-Corruption Agency Guidelines*, Agence française Anticorruption (AFA), Paris, https://www.agence-francaise-anticorruption.gouv.fr/files/2021-03/French%20AC%20Agency%20Guidelines%20.pdf (accessed on 20 September 2021). [4]

Brinkerhoff, D. (2000), "Assessing political will for anti-corruption efforts: an analytic framework", *Public Administration and Development*, Vol. 20, pp. 239-252, http://onlinelibrary.wiley.com/doi/10.1002/1099-162X(200008)20:3%3C239::AID-PAD138%3E3.0.CO;2-3/abstract (accessed on 5 January 2015). [14]

CGU (2018), *Guia Prático de Gestão de Riscos para a Integridade: Orientações para a Administração Pública Federal direta, autárquica e fundacional*, Controladoria Geral da União (CGU), Brasilia, https://www.gov.br/cgu/pt-br/centrais-de-conteudo/publicacoes/integridade/arquivos/manual-gestao-de-riscos.pdf (accessed on 4 August 2021). [10]

CGU (2018), *Guia Prático de Implementação de Programa de Integridade Pública*, Controladoria-Geral da União (CGU), Brasilia, https://www.gov.br/cgu/pt-br/centrais-de-conteudo/publicacoes/integridade/arquivos/integridade-2018.pdf (accessed on 17 August 2021). [1]

CGU (2017), *Como Fortalecer Sua Gestão: Lei Anticorrupção e Programa de Integridade*, Controladoria-Geral da União, Brasilia, https://www.gov.br/cgu/pt-br/centrais-de-conteudo/publicacoes/transparencia-publica/colecao-municipio-transparente/arquivos/como-fortalecer-sua-gestao-lei-anti-corrupcao-e-programa-de-integridade.pdf (accessed on 24 August 2021). [19]

CGU (2017), *Sugestões de Decretos para a regulamentação da Lei Anticorrupção em Municípios*, Controladoria-Geral da União, Brasilia, https://www.gov.br/cgu/pt-br/centrais-de-conteudo/publicacoes/transparencia-publica/colecao-municipio-transparente/arquivos/cartilha-sugestoes-de-decretos-para-a-regulamentacao-da-lei-anticorrupcao-nos-municipios.pdf (accessed on 24 August 2021). [20]

Miller, G. (1955), "The Magical Number Seven, Plus or Minus Two Some Limits on Our Capacity for Processing Information", *Psychological Review*, Vol. 101/2, pp. 343-352, http://www.psych.utoronto.ca/users/peterson/psy430s2001/Miller%20GA%20Magical%20Seven%20Psych%20Review%201955.pdf (accessed on 24 January 2018). [7]

OECD (2020), *Improving Governance with Policy Evaluation: Lessons From Country Experiences*, OECD Public Governance Reviews, OECD Publishing, Paris, https://dx.doi.org/10.1787/89b1577d-en. [21]

OECD (2020), *OECD Public Integrity Handbook*, OECD Publishing, Paris, https://dx.doi.org/10.1787/ac8ed8e8-en. [3]

OECD (2019), *Follow up report on the OECD Integrity Review of Mexico: Responding to citizens' expectations*, OECD, Paris, https://www.oecd.org/gov/ethics/follow-up-integrity-review-mexico.pdf (accessed on 19 August 2021). [15]

OECD (2019), *La Integridad Pública en América Latina y el Caribe 2018-2019: De Gobiernos reactivos a Estados proactivos*, OECD, Paris, https://www.oecd.org/gov/ethics/integridad-publica-en-america-latina-caribe-2018-2019.htm. [9]

OECD (2019), *Offices of Institutional Integrity in Peru: Implementing the Integrity System*, OECD, Paris, https://www.oecd.org/gov/ethics/offices-of-institutional-integrity-peru.pdf (accessed on 19 August 2021). [17]

OECD (2018), *Behavioural Insights for Public Integrity: Harnessing the Human Factor to Counter Corruption*, OECD Public Governance Reviews, OECD Publishing, Paris, https://dx.doi.org/10.1787/9789264297067-en. [6]

OECD (2017), *Monitoring and Evaluating Integrity Policies*, Working Party of Senior Public Integrity Officials GOV/PGC/INT(2017)4, Paris. [5]

OECD (2017), *OECD Integrity Review of Mexico: Taking a Stronger Stance Against Corruption*, OECD Public Governance Reviews, OECD Publishing, Paris, https://dx.doi.org/10.1787/9789264273207-en. [16]

OECD (2017), *OECD Recommendation of the Council on Public Integrity*, http://www.oecd.org/gov/ethics/Recommendation-Public-Integrity.pdf. [2]

OECD (2004), "OECD Guidelines for Managing Conflict of Interest in the Public Service", in *Managing Conflict of Interest in the Public Service: OECD Guidelines and Country Experiences*, OECD Publishing, Paris, https://dx.doi.org/10.1787/9789264104938-2-en. [12]

OECD (forthcoming), *Behavioural Insights for Public Integrity: Strengthening integrity leadership in Brazil's federal executive branch*, OECD Publishing, Paris. [8]

OECD (forthcoming), *Modernising Integrity Risk Management in Brazil*, OECD Publishing, Paris. [11]

OECD (forthcoming), *Open Government Review of Brazil*, OECD Publishing, Paris. [18]

World Bank, O. (2018), *G20 Good Practice Guide: Preventing and Managing Conflicts of Interest in the Public Sector*, Prepared at the request of the G20 Anticorruption Working Group by the World Bank, OECD and UNODC, https://www.unodc.org/documents/corruption/Publications/2020/Preventing-and-Managing-Conflicts-of-Interest-in-the-Public-Sector-Good-Practices-Guide.pdf (accessed on 26 January 2021). [13]

www.ingramcontent.com/pod-product-compliance
Ingram Content Group UK Ltd.
Pitfield, Milton Keynes, MK11 3LW, UK
UKHW051259180426
11947UKWH00020B/1809